Spirit Over

Flesh

OVY ADELEYE M.D

This book addresses everyday issues that are encountered by
pre-teens, adolescents and young adults as they attempt to
live a Spirit filled life. It gives us the perspective from God's
word on how to live as Christians in our ever changing world.

WESTBOW·
PRESS
A DIVISION OF THOMAS NELSON
& ZONDERVAN

Scripture quotations are from The Holy Bible, English Standard
Version® (ESV®), copyright © 2001 by Crossway, a publishing ministry
of Good News Publishers. Used by permission. All rights reserved.

WestBow Press books may be ordered through booksellers or by contacting:

WestBow Press
A Division of Thomas Nelson & Zondervan
1663 Liberty Drive
Bloomington, IN 47403
www.westbowpress.com
1 (866) 928-1240

ISBN: 978-1-4908-6022-0 (sc)
ISBN: 978-1-4908-6023-7 (e)

Library of Congress Control Number: 2014920432

Print information available on the last page.

WestBow Press rev. date: 03/02/2015

Contents

Bible verses will be taken mostly from the English Standard Version of the bible (ESV). Entire proceeds from the sale of this book will contribute to providing literacy and job training skills for widows and youth where no sufficient social structure exists for their development in Nigeria, West Africa. Funds will be donated to the non-profit organization; Foundation for Culture, Youth and Women Empowerment founded by my mother Dr.(Mrs) G.A.E. Makoju.

Special thanks to my Spirit filled sisters, Dr. Jokotade Adeleye and Engr. Onyeche Tifase for their editing, support and encouragement.

Introduction

For those who live according to the flesh set their minds on things of the flesh, but those who live according to the Spirit set their minds on the Spirit. For to set the mind on the flesh is death, but to set the mind on the Spirit is life and peace. For the mind that is set on the flesh is hostile to God, for it does not submit to God's law; indeed it cannot. Those who are in the flesh cannot please God. So then brothers, we are debtors, not to the flesh, to live according to the flesh. For if you live according to the flesh you will die, but if by the Spirit you put to death the deeds of the body, you will live. For all who are led by the Spirit of God are sons of God. For you did not receive the spirit of slavery to fall back into fear, but you have received the Spirit of adoption as sons, by whom we cry, 'Abba! Father!" The Spirit himself bears witness with our spirit that we are children of God, and if children then heirs – heirs of God and fellow heirs with Christ, provided we suffer with him in order that we may also be glorified with him.

Romans 8; 5-8,12-17

As children of the Lord we acknowledge that he is our creator and provider and sincerely desire to fulfill the purpose for which he created us. Our Lord has granted each of us the gift of free will by which we can choose to be obedient to the Holy Spirit or to be obedient to our flesh with its needs and desires. A true love of God means that we surrender ourselves to be led by the Spirit of the Lord that dwells in his word and within us. It is only after we have experienced the transformation of the children of God that we can die to self and be re-born to a new life of obedience in the Spirit. As Christians we must all come to experience the transformation which is the re-birth of the spirit so that we are obedient to the Holy Spirit rather than to our flesh and its needs. As we venture through life we often find ourselves at crossroads where we have to make a choice either to be led by the Spirit or by the flesh. This book hopes to open our eyes to the Lords will as it is clearly stated in his word. We will also come to understand some of the tools the Lord has given us to inform us, instruct us, strengthen us and enable us be re-born of the spirit. It is our Lord's desire that we be united with him each and every day until we meet to part no more at the end of time. Our Lord is our shepherd and as his humble sheep we must answer his call willingly so we experience the transformation of born of flesh to born of spirit.

Let us all answer the call of salvation and come receive the grace that is ours on account of our faith in a risen Christ, so that we are empowered to lay down our flesh and live according to the Spirit. As children of God, we must understand why sin can no longer separate us from our salvation because of the grace earned us by Christ's crucifixion. It is now our faith and not obedience to the Law that earns us the grace freely given by our Lord that grants us our salvation. As children of the light, we have conquered darkness and by the grace of our Lord, sin no longer has power over us. Come, and let us take a walk together for a while as we discover the Spirit, the flesh and the tools available to us as children of God, to win the victory of 'Spirit over Flesh', for only then can we truly be children of God.

Roman's 6:14 for sin will have no dominion over you, since you are not under the law, but under grace.

CHAPTER ONE

Our Creation

Our bodies are made in God's image, this means that we are like God for he made us to be like him.

Genesis 1: 27 -" So God created man in his own image, in the image of God he created him; male and female he created them".

Man is made up of body, soul and spirit. The body is the physical form or flesh, this is the form that we can touch, see and feel. It is our responsibility as individuals to provide all that is necessary to maintain our physical well-being including good nutrition, clothing, shelter and adequate exercise. As children of the spirit we must give up the flesh to death so that we may rise to a new life in the Spirit of Christ.

Man also has a spirit, The Lord breathed into the nostrils of the man He formed (Adam) and he became a living being (Genesis 2:7). The spirit is life in the breath that the Lord gave Adam at the beginning of creation. This life in the breath called spirit is what gives life to the physical flesh. The spirit form in which we exist is not physical; it cannot be seen, touched or felt. The spirit form is the form in which we exist that is like God, this is the form that affords dignity and respect to all man. The Lord created us in his own image, meaning that we are Spirit as our Lord is Spirit, our Lord out of the love he has for us has also given us free will as his children. It is by our own free will that we choose to be called children of God, as children of God this book explores the transformation that empowers us to make the choice of the way of the spirit over the way of the flesh as a fulfillment of our desire to be obedient to our heavenly father. The mere fact that the Lord saw it fit to create each of us as a being, in his own image, surely is reason enough to confirm the love that our Lord has for each and every one of us. This is why all creation, from the time conceived to the time of death, as long as we possess the spirit that gives life is loved by God and worthy of love by all men. It is very important that we understand the dignity of all God's creation and the love that God has for all his creation.

Matthew 5:43-48: "You have heard that it was said, 'you shall love your neighbor and hate your enemy. But I say to you, Love your enemies and pray for those who persecute you, so that you may be sons of your Father who is in heaven. For he makes his sun rise on the evil and on the good, and sends rain on the just and on the unjust. For if you love those who love you, what reward do you have? Do not even the tax collectors do the same? And if you greet only your brothers, what more are you doing than others? Do not even the gentiles do the same? You therefore must be perfect as your heavenly father is perfect."

It is clear that our Lord loves all people, sinner or righteous, just or unjust, able or disabled, evil or good. It is this love that our Lord has for us that caused him to give up his son Jesus Christ as a willing sacrifice, so that we may be saved and reborn to a new life in Christ, for only then can we live in the Spirit and inherit his kingdom.

Romans 5; 8 but God shows his love for us in that while we were still sinners Christ died for us.

We also like Christ, must love all of God's creation without an expectation of reciprocation, for this is what makes us children of God.

Much like the physical form of us is made up of many parts, so also the spirit form in which we exist has its various parts. As we nourish, groom and nurture the physical being, so also we must nourish groom and nurture the spirit. Unfortunately, we often overlook nourishment of the spirit, which can lead to illness, disease and death of the spirit.

Genesis 2: 7 -" Then the Lord God formed the man of dust from the ground, and breathed into his nostrils the breath of life, and man became a living creature".

The spirit within us, which is the 'life in the breath' that gives us life, exists within us from the time of our creation and never experiences a permanent death. As soon as we are conceived, the flesh begins to form, the spirit within us is also formed at our conception, though a mother's breath and blood sustain a child till birth. Once a child is born and takes his first breath of life, he is no longer dependent on his mother for life and sustenance. The miracle of conception much like the miracle of the church shows how we can be separate yet one in spirit, mother, father and child much like the holy trinity, three separate beings yet one in the spirit of the conceived child, we cannot help but marvel at the wonder of God's creation. The physical form in which we exist must experience a final death in the physical world, but our faith as Christians is that we continue to experience life in the hereafter as spirit after our physical death.

The spirit form which exists within us from the time of our conception has inherited the stain of original sin from the disobedience our first father Adam. Our spirit therefore has to be washed clean and experience a re-birth that renews it and causes it to be subject to the Holy Spirit, this is termed being 'born again'. As Christians who possess a spirit that has been born again, we remain aware at all times that our regenerated spirit can fall from grace if we fail to live a life of faith. Once we experience a re-birth of the spirit, the Lord provides us the grace so that we may strive to live in complete obedience to his word. Much like the Holy Spirit descended upon the apostles at Pentecost, so should all Christ's followers desire to receive the Holy Spirit into their hearts to enable them fulfill the purpose for which they are created. As we receive the Holy Spirit our desire is that our spirit is transformed and brought to a new birth. We recognize the re-birth of the spirit form or 'being born again' as the transformation of our spirit by the grace granted us on account of our faith in a resurrected Christ.

God's word informs us severally that to inherit eternal life as a Christian, it is a pre-requisite that our spirit form experience a re-birth.

John 3:3 -" Jesus answered him, "Truly, truly, I say to you, unless one is born again he cannot see the kingdom of God".

John 3:5-8 "Jesus answered, "Truly, truly, I say to you, unless one is born of water and the Spirit, he cannot enter the kingdom of God. That which is born of the flesh is flesh, and that which is born of the Spirit is spirit. Do not marvel that I said to you, you must be born again. The wind blows where it wishes, and you hear its sound, but you do not know where it comes from or where it goes. So it is with everyone who is born of the Spirit."

CHAPTER TWO

The Re-Birth of the Children of God

The body can have several kinds of birth, this birth is synonymous with baptism. Baptism comes from the Greek word baptizien which means immerse. It is only after we have been 'immersed in' or baptized that we can emerge as 'born of'. After we are born of flesh it is necessary for us to voluntarily die to the flesh and its needs, be washed clean and re-born with the water of true repentance and with a new spirit that is of Christ. At the end of time we will either experience the birth by the fire of the final judgment or be delivered to eternal life with our heavenly father. Let us explore the births that we must experience as children of God.

- Firstly to be born of flesh in which we are born of our mother's womb in the physical and have our own individual flesh and spirit on the day of our birth into this world.

- Secondly to be born of water in which we are baptized with water and receive the grace to be called children of God or Christians. It is during baptism by water that we are traditionally immersed in water, this immersion signifies a washing away or cleansing from original sin. At the time of baptism we must present ourselves with a true and contrite heart.

John the Baptist describes water baptism as a baptism with water for repentance in Matthew 3; 11. From the time of the first sin of disobedience committed by our father Adam in the Garden of Eden when he ate of the fruit of the tree of which the Lord had commanded him not to eat, we were no longer in the right with our Lord, our spirit nature had fallen from grace and we were all born with the stain of original sin as is recorded in Genesis Chapter 3. It is by our water baptism that we acknowledge our sinful nature which we inherited from our father Adam, repent of our sinful past and are put right or reconciled with our Heavenly Lord. John the Baptist baptized with water all believers who heeded his call to repentance in preparation to receive the Christ that was to come. The Baptism of John however was only a beginning and preparation of the full restoration that Christ alone was to fulfill, the re-birth of the Spirit.

Water baptism continues to be recognized by most Christian denominations as an outward sign of an inner repentance and an initiation into the Christian faith. There should be no doubt that the water in water baptism is a sign of the cleansing by the Lord that washes us free of the original sin which we inherited from our Father Adam and prepares us for a life free of sin and to be re-born of Spirit as we welcome the Holy Spirit into our hearts. Several Christian denominations now see water baptism as obsolete. Just as we could not be born of the Spirit if we were not first born of the flesh, so also we cannot truly be transformed to children of God if we are not born of water for repentance. Christ himself did not come to remove the laws of our prophets, he only came to bring the work of our salvation to completion so that we would no longer seek salvation by obedience to the law but rather by a faith in a resurrected Christ.

Water baptism though necessary for the spiritual cleansing from original sin that it brings cannot replace the baptism that is of Christ which is baptism by the Holy Spirit. The actual experience of water baptism is spiritual, the physical cleansing by water signifies that our spirit form is cleansed of all sin and can now rise to a new life in Christ without original sin.

Once we are baptized of water, we should be prepared to be born of the Holy Spirit, these events occurred concurrently with Christ when he was baptized at the river Jordan, however these two events can occur in any order as the Spirit pleases and they are both a requirement to inherit eternal life.

• Thirdly to be born of the Holy Spirit, John the Baptist referred to this re-birth of the spirit as the Baptism by the Holy Spirit which was to be of Christ in Matthew 3;11 . The re-birth of the spirit is also termed 'to be born again'. The Holy Spirit once we acknowledge our faith in Christ and his resurrection may come upon us quietly at his will or dramatically as an outpouring as he did at Pentecost. It is when he comes upon us that we are immersed within the Holy Spirit and transformed from 'spirit born of flesh" to 'spirit born of the Holy Spirit." For those who are Apostles of Christ, Priests, helpers or leaders in the church that possess the Holy Spirit, they may also give the Holy Spirit to Christ followers by the laying of hands or the breathing of the Holy Spirit upon their Christian brethren. As Christian believers we also if willed by the Holy Spirit can give the gift of the Holy Spirit to others by the laying of hands or by sharing the word. Once we receive the Holy Spirit within us, he will manifest himself to us by the gifts of the Holy Spirit we come to poses and we will bear the fruits of the Holy Spirit in our lives. As long as we profess a faith in the risen Christ that is true and a desire for the re-birth of our spirit, the Holy Spirit will come upon us and transform us. Christ's Apostles baptized believers in the way that he directed after his death. We must not forget the free will that is our right as children of God for his Spirit will only transform us if we are willing.

Matthew 28; 19 Go therefore and make disciples of all nations, baptizing them in the name of the Father and of the Son and of the Holy Spirit, teaching them to observe all that I have commanded you. And behold, I am with you always, to the end of the age".

It is crucial that we attempt to understand the Baptism that Christ received for only then can we truly emulate Christ as children of God.

Matthew 3: 16 And when Jesus was baptized, immediately he went up from the water. And behold the heavens were opened to him, and he saw the Spirit of God descending like a dove and coming to rest on him; and behold a voice from heaven said "This is my son, with whom I am well pleased."

The baptism by water of Jesus and descent of the Holy Spirit upon him thereafter illustrates a few critical doctrines to us. Firstly,

Christ was humble enough to undergo a water Baptism even though he was without sin, how much more should we who were born in a state of original sin receive the baptism of water. Secondly, Christ was of the Holy Spirit even from the time of his conception for this Spirit existed within him at his creation, yet the Lord sent the Holy Spirit upon him as a dove, how much more we who were born sinners with a Spirit of flesh that often seeks to satisfy the desires of the flesh, need to welcome the Holy Spirit into our hearts and allow him to transform us to be born of his very nature.

Matthew 3: 11 John said; "I baptize you with water for repentance, but he who is coming after me is mightier than I, whose sandals I am not worthy to carry. He will baptize you with the Holy Spirit and fire.

After the baptism by the Holy Spirit we emerge as born of the Holy Spirit. We must share in Christ's death in order that we may die to the flesh and emerge as re-born in the Spirit. As we unite ourselves with Christ unto his death, we die to the flesh and sin and arise to a new life in the Spirit where sin no longer has power over us. We can describe the baptism by the Holy Spirit as a baptism unto death, in as much as we understand that to rise to a new life in the Spirit we must first die to life in the flesh. The Apostle Paul explains the doctrine of 'Baptism by the Holy Spirit', the 'Death to flesh' and 'Rising to a new life in Christ' in the book of Romans.

Roman's 6:3-7, 12-14 Do you know that all of us who have been baptized into Christ Jesus were baptized into his death? We were buried therefore with him by baptism into death, in order that, just as Christ was raised from the dead by the glory of the father, we too might walk in newness of life. For if we have been united with him in a death like his, we shall certainly be united with him in a resurrection like his. We know that our old self was crucified with him in order that the body of sin might be brought to nothing, so that we would no longer be enslaved to sin. For one who has died has been set free from sin. Let not sin therefore reign in your mortal body, to make you obey its passions. Do not present your members to sin as instruments for unrighteousness, but present yourselves to God as those who have been brought from death to life, and your members to God as instruments for righteousness. For sin will have no dominion over you, since you are not under the law but under grace.

This gives rise to a popular question;' If we are no longer subject to the Law, then why do we have to obey the Law, why struggle to overcome sins against the body?' As long as we live under God's grace that becomes available to us on account of the faith we have in a risen Christ, we are no longer subject to sin because our flesh with its passions has been given up to death. Our baptism unto death means that we die to the flesh and rise to live a life that is righteous according to God's purpose, not our own. It is by God's grace that we are willing to die to the flesh and completely surrender to our Lord's will. As baptized Christians we can truly say; "I have presented myself to the Lord in true repentance, he has washed me free of all my sin, I have received the new birth by water unto repentance, I am prepared to die unto Christ in my flesh, so that I may rise to a new life in the Spirit." Baptism by water is the beginning of total surrender a sign of our repentance and the forgiveness we receive. Baptism by the Holy Spirit, a sign that we are prepared for total surrender, no longer slaves to the flesh and sin but rather ready to die to the flesh and come to life in the Spirit unto Christ and righteousness.

Jesus Christ, when he was first baptized by water soon afterwards received the Holy Spirit as an outward apparition in the form of a dove; likewise the apostles received the Holy Spirit as an outward apparition of 'tongues of fire' at Pentecost, there is no doubt that the apostles had been baptized by water prior to Pentecost.

While the Holy Spirit manifests himself to us freely as he wills, once he comes upon us he transforms our spirit of flesh to being born of God's Spirit. It is only after we experience this transformation that we can say we are 'born of the Holy Spirit' or baptized by the Holy Spirit.

Catholics believe that the sacrament of baptism by water also entails a re-birth of the spirit and this occurs when the Priest after pouring water over us in repentance, lays his hands upon the one to be baptized and says the words; receive ye of the Holy Spirit. Some other Christian denominations believe that being born of the spirit which is synonymous with being born again occurs after we repent of our sins and profess our faith, we make ourselves available to the Holy Spirit, so that we can experience the transformation that makes us children of 'The Holy Spirit'. Various Christian denominations have various beliefs on how the spirit within us receives a re-birth. For a re-birth of the spirit to occur an individual has to repent of sin, be willing, waiting and profess his faith in Christ, much like the apostles waiting on the Holy Spirit that arrived to them at Pentecost. The re-birth of the spirit is however not an event that we can control as the Holy Spirit moves freely and as he pleases, the time or place where he chooses to present himself we cannot predict. It is our faith as Christians that our Lord's greatest desire is that each of us his sheep will return unto him the good shepherd, voluntarily by our own free will. Out of the great love that the Lord has for us he has created us and allowed us to freely roam the pasture of the world, the freedom is ours to choose to return to Christ and die to the flesh so as to be re-born in the spirit. If we have a true love for our Lord and master we must lay down our lives and return to him as he awaits and searches for each and every one of us his chosen people. It is only after a death to self and rising to a new life in the spirit that we can say we have presented ourselves as true worthy sheep to our shepherd.

Acts 2: 3-4 And divided tongues as of fire appeared to them and rested on each one of them. And they were all filled with the Holy Spirit, and began to speak in other tongues as the spirit gave them utterance.

There is no doubt that as the Holy Spirit descended upon the apostles at Pentecost he transformed them by a re-birth of their spirit. The Baptism by the Holy Spirit does not make the baptism by water obsolete, both events simply are a completion of each other as we come full circle in our lives as Christians. How can we be born of the Holy Spirit if we do not first acknowledge that we are sinners and repent of our sin? Today, as at the time of John, many still need to heed the call to repentance and take the straight path that leads to Christ. The good news is that they are no longer just called to repentance and baptism by water but also to a baptism of the Holy Spirit. We all receive of the fullness of living waters and are called to experience, repentance, forgiveness of sin, the outpouring of the Holy Spirit, death to flesh and sin, rising to a new life in the Spirit and the re-birth of our spirit within. This is the full circle, the call of Jesus Christ to which we each must answer, John the Baptist himself could only allude to this call for it was Christ alone that would bring the entire circle to completion.

It is important to understand how baptism by water and baptism by the Holy Spirit work together to make us whole as Christians. We cannot truly say we are Christian or part of God's family if we are not born of water and born of the Spirit.

As Christians, nothing else is required on our part for a re-birth of the spirit to occur save that we repent of our sins, believe in our hearts and profess with our mouths that Jesus is Lord and that he died in reparation for our sins and that God raised him from the dead. Our Faith is all that is needed and we shall be immersed in the Holy Spirit as he descends upon us and transforms us as we emerge with our spirit re-born.

Romans 10:9 because, if you confess with your mouth that Jesus is Lord and believe in you heart that God raised him from the dead, you will be saved.

If this faith we have is true then we must surrender ourselves fully to the Holy Spirit and allow the spirit within us from the time of our birth to die and be re-born of the Holy Spirit. This will result in a transformation of our spirit from being born of flesh to being born of the Holy Spirit. If our Spirit is born of the Holy Spirit, then we have voluntarily given up ourselves, died to ourselves and totally submitted to the Holy Spirit that he may transform the spirit within us and lead us as he wills.

Galatians 2: 19-21 For through the law I died to the law so that I might live for God. I have been crucified with Christ. It is no longer

I who live, but Christ lives in me. And the life I now live in the flesh, I live by faith in the Son of God, who loved me and gave himself for me. I do not nullify the grace of God, for if righteousness were through the law, then Christ died for no purpose.

There is no doubt that by tradition the water must be present during baptism by water. While the water is only an outward sign of the cleansing of the spirit form, the act of cleansing is spiritual. Provided the intent and desire to die to sin and rise to new life in Christ, the water need not be present for baptism to occur. However, once water is available it is appropriate to use water as an outward sign of the spiritual cleansing from original sin. Christ had no need to be baptized for he was without sin, there is no doubt that he upheld the tradition John had begun and underwent the cleansing by water as a sign to us who wish to be obedient to his word. We cannot claim to be Christians or Christ-like and have no desire to be like him. If Christ was humble enough to be baptized, anyone who calls himself Christian should be humble and respectful enough to be baptized. It is required by our doctrine as Christian

Just as an athlete prepares his body for a race or competition, so must a Christian prepare his spirit to be welcomed into God's kingdom. The spirit within us must experience a re-birth for us to inherit God's kingdom, as Jesus Christ said "Except a man be born of spirit and of water he cannot enter God's kingdom". We may profess this desire to receive the Holy Spirit and for a re-birth of our Spirit to occur, but we must look unto our Lord and wait expectantly for him to grant us his grace. Not all people will have a dove descend upon them or tongues of fire settle upon them, but once we receive Holy Spirit and experience the re-birth of our spirit we are filled with God's grace, empowered to prophesy his word and manifest some form of gift from the Holy Spirit, such as; wisdom, knowledge, faith, healing, working of miracles, prophesy, discernment of spirits, speaking in tongues, interpretation of tongues and we bear the fruits of the spirit in our character by our love, joy, peace, forbearance, kindness, goodness, faithfulness, gentleness and self-control.

Acts 2; 38-39 And Peter said to them, "Repent and be baptized, every one of you, in the name of Jesus Christ for the forgiveness of your sins, and you will receive the gift of the Holy Spirit. For the promise is for you and your children and all who are far off – everyone who the Lord our God calls to himself."

Note the words repent and be baptized as this further confirms that we must be baptized unto repentance which signifies the baptism by water and then also be baptized unto the Holy Spirit in the name of Jesus Christ to inherit the kingdom of God.

The question might then be, are not all men called, or is the Holy Spirit only reserved for God's chosen people. If we understand the love that God has for all men then this question should not arise. We are all God's chosen people, sinner or righteous and as long as we have faith in the risen Christ; Paul tells us to repent and be baptized and we will all receive the gift of the Holy Spirit, for he has been promised freely to all. Not all who have received the gift of the Holy Spirit will experience an earth shattering manifestation in the physical sense, we will however experience a transformation of our spirit self, which will cause us to yield the fruit of the Holy Spirit in our lives. It is only after we have experienced this transformation that we can live a life of the Spirit.

• The fourth kind of birth we can experience is to be born of fire; at the end of time we will be judged, this fire will consume the chaff from the wheat. The baptism of fire is one that will occur at the time of the final judgment. Those who are worthy will receive eternal life in our Lord's kingdom but, those who are found wanting will be engulfed in an un-quenching fire.

As modern day Christians we often refer to trials and tribulations as a refiner's fire, this implies that we have endured these trials and tribulations and emerged unscathed or even further strengthened and transformed by the Spirit. It is only by the grace of the Lord that we can conquer, destroy and emerge even further strengthened from these trials. The fire of the final judgment is however reserved for those who have refused to be transformed by the spirit and choose to fulfil the desires of the flesh as they present themselves. If we refuse to die to the flesh and its needs we are invariably choosing the baptism of fire over the baptism of the Holy Spirit, the choice is ours to make freely.

The words of John the Baptist in Matthew 3: 10-11 Even now the axe is laid to the root of the trees. Every tree therefore that does not bear good fruit is cut down and thrown into the fire. "I baptize you with water for repentance, but he who is coming after me is mightier than I, whose sandals I am not worthy to carry. He will baptize you with the Holy Spirit and fire. His winnowing fork is in his hand, and he will clear his threshing floor, gathering his wheat into the barn and burning up the chaff with un-quenchable fire."

To understand that the wheat has to be separated from the chaff, means that we understand that the believers have to be separated from the unbelievers at the final judgment. I hate to use the term believers and unbelievers because this signifies that all believers are born of the spirit, which is false. As children of God so many of us have a faith in the one true God and his son Jesus Christ our Lord, but yet refuse to die to the flesh and choose instead to indulge its every request and need as much as they are against the desire of the Holy Spirit. Those who on account of their faith have died to the flesh and no longer allow sin rule them are made worthy wheat, if we choose to remain subject to the flesh and choose not to make ourselves useful according to our Lord's purpose, then we have chosen to be useless chaff that will be consumed by the fire of the final judgment.

Hebrews 10: 26 -27 For if we go on sinning deliberately after receiving the knowledge of the truth, there no longer remains a sacrifice for sins, but a fearful expectation of judgment and a fury of fire that will consume the adversaries.

Our life as Christians should have one ultimate goal, and that is eternal life with our heavenly Father in his heavenly kingdom. It is only after we have received the baptism by water and the baptism by the Holy Spirit that our spirit can truly achieve this ultimate goal; if we remain of the flesh then we live according to desires of the flesh and cannot have the grace to overcome the flesh and be subject to the Spirit. This very nature of a life of righteousness is made available to us only by the grace that our faith earns us, and we will further explore the grace that our faith earns us in Chapter Sixteen - Faith and God's Grace.

CHAPTER THREE

Spirit; Heart, Soul, Mind and Will

When the Lord created us, he created us as flesh and spirit. The spirit form within us was created in God's image, however the disobedience of Adam and Eve in the Garden of Eden, separated us from God. It is the re-birth by water and the Holy Spirit that causes a transformation for us to begin to return to spirit in God's image.

Christ says in John 3:6 That which is born of the flesh is flesh, and that which is born of the Spirit is spirit.

Just as the body has its various parts so also our spirit has various parts some of which are;

• The thought which is the spirit form within us in which we contemplate our circumstances and actions. It is only after we have contemplated in our thoughts that we determine our actions and carry them out by our own free will.

• The heart which is the spirit form in which our emotions are determined such as love hate, envy, anger, and jealousy.

• The will which is the spirit form that permits our thoughts and emotions to become actions and words after we have contemplated in our mind.

• The mind can be described as the residence of our thoughts.

• The soul is the seat of our spirit form where the ego and conscience exist and do battle to determine our own will and preferred actions.

There is no question that our actions and emotions are subject to our will, and no doubt that we must determine in which accord our will directs our actions and words. It is only after we have contemplated in our thoughts that we act by our own free will. Our transformation as children of God means that the spirit within us is transformed from spirit that is obedient to the flesh to spirit that is obedient to the Holy Spirit. In situations where we have chosen a course of action that is against the will of the Holy Spirit, he again directs us in our conscience, we are again free to act as the Holy Spirit directs our conscience if we so choose. Certain individuals however give up their will or spirit and allow their thoughts and actions be influenced by drugs, alcohol, the will and direction of others or the desires of the flesh. Once we submit our will to be directed by any other than the Holy Spirit we have chosen the way of the flesh and must remain accountable for our actions. It is important that we guard our spirit form, nurture it with the word of God, rather than the words or thoughts of non-believers lest we surrender to the flesh and its needs. Let us also understand that as much as the Lord speaks to us in his word, the word of God is Spirit.The word of God has the ability to influence our Spirit form in our thoughts and our will, and then in turn direct our physical form by our actions and emotions.

John 6: 63 - It is the Spirit who gives life, the flesh is no help at all. The words that I have spoken to you are spirit and life.

• The word, once we hear it in our ears, has access to our thoughts and mind in our spirit form hence there is no doubt that the word is spirit. As Christians we believe that the word existed from the beginning of creation when the Lord created the entire world by his word. We also believe that the word came to be flesh in the form of Jesus Christ, these are mysteries of the Spirit which only he can reveal. The word can influence our thoughts by giving us a standard by which to measure our thoughts and actions, we then by our own free will act according to the word, hence the word has transformed us. As we live in a world that is so infused with technology and the media there is a danger of our conscience being infused by what it learns from our environment. This can be detrimental because the way of the world is not always the way of our Lord which is clearly stated in his word. The word causes us to act in God's precepts, we however have to be willing to let God's will be done, as believers we have to allow it. This is the freedom that we have as children of God that our will prevails in all situations, our Lord never forces our hand when we act. The word dwells in our thoughts once we have heard it and is the yardstick within us that directs our conscience, it teaches us, corrects us, consoles us and brings us hope and life. There is no doubt that the word is spirit, and is one of the greatest tools that nourishes our spirit.

Hebrews 4;12 For the word of God is living and active, sharper than any two-edged sword, piercing to the division of soul and of spirit, of joints and of marrow, and discerning the thoughts and intentions of the heart.

• The conscience is the spirit within us that gives us the consciousness of what is sin. Our conscience gets its directive from the Spirit of God, the word of God and from our environment as to what is perceived as sinful or righteous. We must not underestimate how our culture and environment directs our conscience. The media and popular culture often feed our conscience with the perspective of the world on controversial matters. We must always remember that the only way to win the victory of Spirit over flesh is to always choose the way of the Spirit over the way of popular culture. This is what makes us children of God. Our conscience is the spirit form within us that judges our thoughts and actions, bringing them to our consciousness and it came at a dear price...

Genesis 2: 17 but of the tree of the knowledge of good and evil, you shall not eat, for in the day that you eat of it you shall surely die."

It is only after Adam and Eve had been disobedient to our Lord and eaten of the forbidden tree that they came to a consciousness of good and evil. Their disobedience did not cause a death of their flesh but rather a death of their spirit, this was the consequence of their sin. But the Lord still despite their disobedience did not leave them to their own devices; he gave them the spirit form in their conscience to judge their thoughts and actions.

• The ego is the spirit of flesh that panders to the needs of the flesh and satisfies its every need. The spirit of our ego is not of the Holy Spirit but rather of our human nature. The ego causes us to excuse our sinful nature, live in denial and justify our sin. As children of God when we choose to die to the flesh and be re-born in the spirit we have declared that we are no longer subject to the ego but rather choose to be led by the voice of the Spirit of God in our conscience.

Romans 2: 15 – They show that the work of the law is written on their hearts, while their conscience also bears witness, and their conflicting thoughts accuse or even excuse them.

The accusing thoughts would be the conscience and the excusing thoughts would be the ego. Every time we choose evil over good, every time we are disobedient to God's word, we kill the life giving spirit within us. We have the spirit form of conscience within us as the knowledge of good and evil, unfortunately despite this knowledge we often by our own free will go against what is good, and listen to our ego with its conflicting thoughts, resulting in sin which brings us death in the spirit.

Hebrews 10: 16 – "This is the covenant that I will make with them after those days, declares the Lord; I will put my laws on their hearts, and write them on their minds."

With God's word in our hearts, minds and thoughts, by our own free will we can choose to be obedient or disobedient, the choice is ours to make freely. As Christians, we must evangelize by sharing God's word, the word gives us fuel in the spirit of our conscience to live our lives according to God's purpose. It is our duty as Spirit filled Disciples of Christ to evangelize by sharing God's spirit in his word as food for his sheep, to instruct and transform others, this is how we show the love we have for our Lord Jesus Christ.

John 21: 17 He said to him the third time "Simon son of John, do you love me?" Peter was hurt because Jesus asked him the third time, "Do you love me?" He said, Lord, you know all things; you know that I love you." Jesus said, "Feed my sheep."

CHAPTER FOUR

My Body, Temple

John 14: 23 – Jesus replied, "Anyone who loves me will obey my teaching. My Father will love them, and we will come to them and make our home with them.

As a true child of God my body becomes a temple of the Lord, a holy place, a worthy dwelling for my Lord Jesus Christ and the Holy Spirit, because the Lord created me to be his holy temple.

1 Corinthians 3: 16-17 Do you not know that you are God's temple and that God's Spirit dwells in you? If anyone destroys God's temple, God will destroy him. For God's temple is holy, and you are that temple.

Indeed my body must be a place of love, peace and tranquility if it is to be worthy as a sanctuary for my Lord. Each individual must understand that they are created to be God's temple. This causes us all to be worthy of the respect and dignity given the sons of God, from the time of our creation until our death. We are each created for this very purpose the word of God gives evidence that we are God's temple. As children of God, the Lord as he pleases dwells in each of us as Spirit. Baptism by water and the Holy Spirit makes us worthy to be God's holy temple for we are washed free of original sin, die to the flesh and rise to a new life in the Spirit. By the re-birth of the Spirit we experience a transformation of our spirit from 'of flesh' to 'of the Holy Spirit' and we now by our Lord's grace are dead to the flesh and obedient to our Lord and his teachings. This faith that we have in a risen Christ is what earns us the grace to be temples of the Holy Spirit. Just as temples and Churches were built as places worthy for our Lord's tabernacle to reside, so are we to prepare and keep ourselves as worthy temples for our Lord. The Holy Spirit is alive and active as God within us, by sharing God's word, his body and blood we are nourishing the Holy Spirit within us.

1 Corinthians 6:19-20 Or do you not know that your body is a temple of the Holy Spirit within you, whom you have from God? You are not your own, for you were bought with a price. So glorify God in your body.

The Apostle Simon Peter made it clear in the Book of Acts that many Christians who had received the Holy Spirit were yet to be baptized with water, and to be a worthy temple we must strive to receive the baptism of water as well as the baptism of the Holy Spirit. It is only as we repent of our sin, die to our flesh and rise to a new life in Christ that we become worthy temples, not by obedience to the law.

Acts 10: 44-47 While Peter was saying these things, the Holy Spirit fell on all who heard the word. And the believers from among the circumcised who had come with Peter were amazed, because the gift of the Holy Spirit was poured out even on the Gentiles. For they were speaking in tongues and extolling God. Then Peter declared, "Can anyone withhold water for baptizing these people, who have received the Holy Spirit just as we have? And he commanded them to be baptized in the name of Jesus Christ.

As soon as we are born of water and the Holy Spirit we are transformed, we receive his gifts and bear his fruits then we can truly say we are God's temple and he is well pleased with us.

1Cor 12: 8-11 To one there is given through the Spirit a message of wisdom, to another a message of knowledge by means of the Spirit, to another faith by the same Spirit, to another the gift of healing by that one spirit, to another miraculous powers, to another prophecy, to another distinguishing between spirits, to another speaking in different kinds of tongues, and to still another the interpretation of tongues. All these are the work of one and the same Spirit, and he distributes them to each one, just as he determines.

Galatians 5:22-23 But the fruit of the Spirit is love, joy, peace, forbearance, kindness, goodness, faithfulness, gentleness and self-control. Against such things there is no law.

As we share God's word and remain obedient to his commands by the grace he grants us, the Holy Spirit blows as he will and will present himself to us in his own time. When the apostles laid their hands on the believers they also granted them the gift of the Holy Spirit so we also must present ourselves to our Apostles, Priests, Pastors and leaders in the church who are filled with the Holy Spirit, that they may pray for us and lay their hands upon us to fill us with the Holy Spirit as he wills it. We must allow the Holy Spirit transform our spirit from within. We cannot say we are of the Spirit if we have no love for our Lord and for our neighbor, if we have no joy in our hearts and are unkind, if we cannot bear difficulty and have no endurance, if we are aggressive and cannot exercise self-control. If we resort to despair and frustration when faced with life's challenges then we must pray for the gift of the Holy Spirit that our character may bear witness to his presence within us.

Acts 8:15,17 When they arrived, they prayed for the new believers there that they might receive the Holy Spirit. Then Peter and John placed their hands on them, and they received the Holy Spirit.

CHAPTER FIVE

Christ's Body, his Church

As much as we are aware that we are created as God's temple, so also we must understand that we are part of the body of Christ. Christ's body is one with our very being. Christ dwells within each of his children in several forms, three of which are; Christ in his word; Christ in the breath of the Spirit; and Christ in his actual body, his body and blood that give life.

1 Corinthians 12: 12-14 For just as the body is one and has many members, and all the members of the body, though many, are one body, so it is with Christ. For in one Spirit we were all baptized into one body – Jews or Greeks, slaves or free – and all were made to drink of one Spirit.

As an individual person each of us remain an important part of the sanctity of the body of Christ because, we are one in the Spirit of Christ. The same Holy Spirit in which we are baptized dwells within each Christian, making us one in the Spirit of Christ. It is this same one Holy Spirit in which we are all baptized that makes us one body and one spirit in Christ. After a hip fracture sustained in a fatal car wreck which I survived only by the grace of God, I have received revelations from Christ that cause me to understand my body better, my body as well as the body of Christ himself and his church. If my hip hurts though my injury is restricted to my hip, then my whole body hurts. One part of the body affects the entire body, be it a little finger, a whole leg, the origin of pain becomes insignificant because the whole body experiences the pain. So it is with the body of Christ, if one part of the body loses its sanctity then the whole body has lost its sanctity, if one part of the body experiences distress then the whole body is in distress. One must not underestimate the importance of oneself and how one affects the whole body of Christ which is Christ himself, his holy church, his chosen people. Every single part of the body is important, we all matter and are equally truly loved by Christ.

The Lord himself as he gave us his Spirit, loved us so completely that he gave us his flesh also so that we may completely be one with him just as he is one with his Father. This great miracle makes us one with God the Father, the Son and the Holy Spirit. Elevating us to the level of being one with the Lord in Spirit, for if we remember that God made us in his own image then surely he made us to be one with him and pleasing to him at the beginning of time. At the beginning our creation we are one with the Lord, sin separated us from this union but in Christ's death he again unites us to be one with him as he gives us his Spirit and his flesh.

Christ validates my existence, causing me to be worthy of his grace and consequently making me worthy so that he may dwell within me. Just as I belong to Christ, he trusts me enough that he gives himself to me. Christ is mine to love, care for, and honor, mine to respect, trust and obey. I have to value myself and understand my value as a member of Christ's body and as his holy temple. It is only in understanding one's role as a member of the body of Christ and one's being as Christ's holy temple that one can begin to understand how sins against the body have far reaching consequences beyond oneself as a being. Sins against the body cause death to the Spirit form that gives everlasting life within an individual not to the physical form. Sins against an individual body affect the entire body of Christ, Christ himself and every member of his body or church, as we are all united with him as one in the same Holy Spirit.

1 Cor 12; 24-27 But God has so composed the body, giving greater honor to the part that lacked it, that there may be no division in the body, but that the members may have the same care for one another. If one member suffers, all suffer together, if one member is honored, all rejoice together. Now you are the body of Christ and individually members of it.

A common misconception is this, 'when I sin against my body I have hurt no one, save myself' or as an ordinary member of the church and not a church leader, my sin does not matter. The word of God corrects this misconception. For if we are one body in Christ we must understand that each of us is indispensable and necessary, every one of us is an integral part of the body of Christ. As children of God when we choose the way of the flesh, we cause pain not only to our very selves, but pain to the entire body of Christ which is his church, and pain to Christ himself who is one with us. Each time we indulge the flesh, we cause the devil and his cohorts to rejoice at another victory, we cause death to our spirit form, we hurt the body of Christ, we drive another nail into the palm of Christ's hand and we pierce him in the side with another spare, each time, again and again, each time.

Sins against the body cause death to our Spirit form, separate us from Christ's body his church and from Christ himself and his love. There is no doubt that from the beginning of creation sin has separated us from God's love and the glory for which he created us. This is why, if we choose sin over righteousness, we have chosen death over life and allow ourselves to continue to be separated from our Father, as children of God we must choose life in the spirit over the flesh.

We must always remember that it is our Baptism in the one same Spirit of Christ that makes us one family of brothers and sisters in Christ.

CHAPTER SIX

The Way of the Flesh

James 1: 14-15 But each person is tempted when he is lured and enticed by his own desire. Then desire when it has conceived gives birth to sin, and sin when it is fully grown brings forth death.

An intimate relationship for a Christian is permissible only between married individuals, for the pleasure it brings and the act of procreation whereby we co-create with our Lord. As individuals, if we willingly partake of fornication or adultery this is not in keeping with life in the Spirit of God. Our Lord is ever ready to forgive us if we repent and seek to do his will and this is why we must not allow sins of the flesh separate us from the salvation that Christ's death earned us.

It is important to recognize the sequence that leads to sins of the flesh, so as to live in the Spirit as children of God. Sins of the flesh serve as a means to separate us from Christ and silence the Spirit form within us in the form of our conscience. Once the conscience is silenced, that act which at a time was unsavory, distasteful or appalling suddenly becomes acceptable. Once bodily sin silences the conscience within us, we repeat the bodily sin with no apprehension. The flesh without the Spirit to judge it, guide it or cause it to conform loses all sense of judgment. We then become slaves to the flesh and derive such pleasure from indulging the flesh, albeit temporarily, that we often find ourselves repeatedly committing these sinful acts to try and prolong or re-experience the pleasure we desire. We can then become desperate enough to perform sinful acts not just of our flesh but against others in order to experience these sinful pleasures.

In Paul's first letter to the Corinthians he states in Chapter 9: 25 - Every athlete in training submits to strict discipline, in order to be crowned with a wreath that will not last, but we do it for one that will last forever. That is why I run straight for the finish line and that is why I am like a boxer who does not waste his punches. I harden my body with blows and bring it under complete control, to keep myself from being disqualified after having called others to the contest.

The crown we are vying for is eternal life, an everlasting gift. That is why we strive to fight against indulging in sins of the flesh. Why bother you say, why not give in or give up? The answer is because failure is not an option, gaining the whole world achieves nothing, and our ultimate goal is to be united with our heavenly father now and at the end of time. The choice is ours to make, give in and indulge in all earthly pleasures and face the consequences at the end of time or live in the Spirit now and earn peace, eternal life, and everlasting joy in the Lord's heavenly kingdom at the end of time.

Sins against the body often begin in the senses of our desire and emotions, and then once our spirit is willing come to fulfillment in the action of our physical bodies. More specifically desire begins in the sense of sight and what we see that we find appealing, also the sense of hearing and speaking and what we say or hear that awakens our feelings of desire and lastly but not the least the sense of touch and sensations that are awakened is where desire is born. Visual stimulation might be in the form of other persons we find desirable, pornography in the form of magazines, videos, T.V or on the internet, once we indulge in a visually appealing form it leads to a pleasurable emotion, desire of a sensual nature, at this point the will or mind becomes involved. At any point where we become aware of a desire for sensual gratification a decision has to be made; do we stifle desire and walk away, or do we dwell on our desire and further fuel it by continuing to indulge our thoughts. If our ego defeats our conscience we decide to take things a step further towards fulfilling our sensual gratification and this usually occurs in a secluded location. All sins of the body occur in some form of isolation or privacy where sensual desire is further aroused and ultimately culminates in fulfillment of sensual gratification. We should recognize that all sensual desire gains access to our hearts through our senses, thoughts and emotions, this means that we must guard our senses. As Christians we guard our senses so as not to put ourselves in inappropriate situations which allow the desire for sensual gratification to rear its head.

After we have begun to have sensual feelings for an individual, if we consent to being isolated then there is a high chance of engaging in foreplay and eventually seeking sensual gratification. Consenting to isolation means placing ourselves in an environment where we face the risk of falling into the temptation of indulging the flesh.

It is important that we understand that isolation is required for most acts of sins of the flesh. Once we are isolated and partake in foreplay, we allow ourselves to be in a state of arousal, and are more likely to fall into the temptation of sensual indulgence. If we have no desire to fall into the temptation of adultery or fornication then we must always engage in public or in the presence of a third party. Passing through the door into seclusion we must be aware of the temptations that we might face and it behooves us to be accompanied by a chaperone to serve as a buffer that can tame the flame of sensual desire before it rears its head. A chaperone is considered an individual who supervises young adults during social interactions. In situations where adolescents or adults are not chaperoned then fornication or adultery may become a temptation, due to the isolation or seclusion that is possible without a chaperone. There is no doubt that the place to check your attitude is at the door, once you venture in thorough he door, it might be too late to check yourself and question your thoughts and intentions.

We all should remain aware that once we consent to isolation or seclusion, this can be inferred by others to mean one is consenting to sensual gratification. It is vital that we communicate clearly at all times so as not to be misunderstood. Many individuals have been raped or abused simply because they knowingly consented to isolation with a person of the opposite sex and had no intention of fornication or adultery. Seclusion with an individual of the opposite sex without the required communication is greatly discouraged. Once an individual consents and participates in the an act of adultery or fornication then we are indulging the needs of the flesh and not living in accordance with the Spirit of our Lord. If an individual is forced to have sexual intercourse against their will without voluntary consent, this is rape, a criminal act and should immediately be reported to legal authorities. No person should tolerate rape out of a fear of stigmatization or shame of publicity. Individuals in a relationship outside of marriage who wish to live accordingly in the way of the Spirit have to be aware of the risk of fornication if they isolate themselves. Christian adolescents have to communicate their intent to live in the Spirit and partake only in social interaction that is uplifting to our spirit as Christians. Giving up the flesh means giving up any of our desires that are not in keeping with a life in the Spirit and if we cannot do this then we are not worthy of being called children of God. When we give up our needs we die to the flesh and choose to use our body for God's glory, this is how we should live as children of God.

Young adults during courtship or social interaction are encouraged to interact as groups and engage in activities that do not require isolation but can occur in public places such as sports, study groups, restaurants, movies, skating rinks, malls and other public places. It would not be appropriate for adolescents in a relationship to meet privately in a bedroom, house or hotel without a chaperone if they desire to live in the Spirit of Christ.

1 Corinthians 6: 18 - Avoid immorality! Any other sin a man commits does not affect his body but the man who is guilty of sexual immorality, sins against his own body. Don't you know that your body is the temple of the Holy Spirit, who lives in you and who was given to you by God? You do not belong to yourselves but to God; he paid a price for you so use your body for God's glory.

CHAPTER SEVEN

Shame or Guilt

1 John 1: 9-10 If we confess our sins, he is faithful and just to forgive us our sins and to cleanse us from all unrighteousness. If we say we have not sinned, we make him a liar and his word is not in us.

Shame can be described as a feeling of guilt for having committed a sinful act that results from our conscience judging us. Shame can be uplifting in that it puts us unto a path of reconciliation with our Lord by leading us to true repentance. It can cause us to reconsider our actions and admit to the error of our ways, we may then make one of two decisions; repent of our action or justify our actions.

• Shame can lead us to true repentance. When we let our conscience judge us, recognize that we have sinned, confess to the Lord, repent of our sin, ask for forgiveness, and make a sincere commitment not to sin again then shame has led to true repentance. It is only if we are truly repentant and will make all efforts not to sin again that we can receive complete forgiveness. As with the adulterous woman, the Lord's response "Go and sin no more" in John 8;11 is evidence that forgiveness is granted with the assumption that there is an intention on the part of the sinner to sin no more. This is not a guarantee that we will sin no more, as we are all sinful by nature, but the intent has to be there to make all efforts to sin no more.

• Shame can lead to denial. When we let the ego convince us that we have done no wrong and instead of repent begin to justify our actions, then we have chosen a state of denial over truth, flesh over Spirit. If we consciously war against our conscience, refuse to repent and ask for forgiveness, choosing rather to justify our actions by whatever theory we can come up with then the ego has defeated the conscience. We might choose to go to war with our conscience and reassure ourselves with our ego by saying... it was not my fault, I was born this way, it is genetic, my father was this way, I was abused as a child, God made me this way to lust after pornography, it is natural - all guys do this, everyone is doing it. The list of excuses we might come up with abounds, every time we justify our sinful actions the ego has defeated our conscience.

• Shame can also lead to a state of despair and this is not of the Spirit of our Lord because it causes us to believe that we are unworthy of forgiveness, and that despite our confession and true act of contrition we cannot receive forgiveness from our Lord. This shame that leads to despair might cause us to think that the sin we have committed is too great to be forgiven, that we have forever separated ourselves from our salvation and that we have been judged to final damnation. Such a sense of despair leads to a death of the Spirit, a desolation, a depression and a loss of a sense of worthiness and self-worth. It is this kind of despair that leads us to question God's love for us and deters us from receiving the absolution from sin that Christ freely gives us. This kind of despair can cause us to turn our backs on our faith and cause us to curse our creator. If we find ourselves in such a state of despair, then it is paramount that we seek help from respected family members who are filled with the Spirit, Pastors or Priests in the church and qualified professionals to counsel us. It is by the grace of the Holy Spirit and by our will that we must accept that God's love for us is true and that his forgiveness holds no grievance as long as our repentance is true. Whenever we find ourselves at such a crossroad of despair in our lives, we must call upon our Lord and with a true sense of hope, we must arise and return to the house of our Father like the prodigal son did in Luke 15; 11-32.

We have defined our conscience as the spirit within us, under the influence of the Spirit of God that judges our actions. We know right from wrong because the Spirit which is God in our conscience judges us, before the act is committed and after. We have also defined the ego as the spirit within us which is of the flesh, the ego seeks to satisfy the needs and the desires of the flesh and is quick to justify the desires and needs of the flesh. When we go to war within ourselves the conscience goes to war with the ego within us, the choice is ours whether we decide to indulge the desires of our flesh or be obedient to the Spirit of God within us in our conscience.

We must not allow shame separate us from our salvation which awaits us. We must not allow shame cause us to question God's love and his forgiveness which he gives freely and willingly. Rather we must let shame cause us to be repentant, ever trusting in our Lord's mercy and compassion and realize that all we require to live according to God's word is his grace which is granted freely. Christ is ever willing and ready to grant us his grace, all that he asks is that we give up our sinful ways die to the flesh and surrender to him, once we willingly receive God's grace we no longer live in sin. Shame is a signal to all believers that it is time for confession of sin, contrition and a true repentance, it is also time to accept the Lord's forgiveness, which we must never question so that we may return to a state of grace.

As long as we remain in a state of despair after a true confession of sin and repentance then we have not come to a full realization of the forgiveness we have received from our Lord. As children of Christ, we must recognize that this type of shame that causes despair can cause us to question God's love, God's mercy, God's compassion, God's forgiveness and our worthiness for salvation. This kind of shame that leads to despair can put us in a state of depression and at risk of self- harm or suicide. This is a very dangerous situation as our life in the Spirit and our physical life are now under threat. Any person that finds themselves in such a state of despair that they cannot begin to accept our Lord's forgiveness must understand that it is past time to ask for help. If we truly have faith in the Lord and believe that salvation is earned us by the grace we received from Christ's death and resurrection, not by obedience to the Law then we have to accept Christ's mercy and compassion as he forgives us and we resolve to sin no more. Let old things be passed away as we resolve to submit to the Spirit and not the flesh, we must never question Christ's mercy. If we remember that Christ was willing to die for us even when we were sinners then we must remember that he is forever willing to forgive us and welcome us back into his fold when we are repentant.

2 Corinthians 5; 17-20 Therefore if anyone is in Christ, he is a new creation. The old has passed away; behold the new has come. All this is from God, who through Christ reconciled us to himself and

gave us the ministry of reconciliation; that is, in Christ God was reconciling the world to himself, not counting their trespasses against them, and entrusting to us the message of reconciliation.

We must not allow the shame of sin cause us to be subject to our ego and inadvertently lead us to deny or falsely justify our actions but rather shame should cause us to experience true contrition, repentance, conversion and reconciliation as we listen to our conscience which leads us to return to Christ on the cross as he awaits us with open arms. No sin is great enough to separate us from the love of Christ except we allow it. As brothers and sisters in Christ we must not fail to ask for help from leaders in the church, our pastors, family members that are filled with the wisdom of the Spirit or mental health professionals when we struggle with despair or depression.

CHAPTER EIGHT

The Way of the Cross

Luke 9; 23-25 And he said to all, "If anyone would come after me, let him deny himself and take up his cross daily and follow me. For whoever would save his life would lose it, but whoever loses his life for my sake will save it. For what does it profit a man if he gains the whole world and loses or forfeits himself?

As Christians we often go through trials and tribulations in life that can be termed a cross, struggle, spiritual warfare or battle. As Christians, we battle against trials and temptation that may cause us to choose the way of the flesh over the way of the Spirit. The battle occurs within our spirit form as we struggle to live in obedience to God's will which is stated clearly in his word and within us in our conscience. It is after a struggle that we make a decision in our mind that we will carry out by our own free will and by God's grace. God's grace is the ultimate gift he has given us to enable us be victorious over every struggle we face. Each time we choose the way of the Spirit when we face a struggle then we have chosen the way of the cross. The devil takes no pleasure in our obedience to God and will often send temptation our way to distract us from our ultimate goal. Temptations may come our way through any of our senses, our thoughts and desires or through other individuals. This is why we must be alert and sober, ever ready to win the battle and carry our cross, the grace of the Lord is always sufficient once we desire to do God's will.

For the word of the cross is folly to those who are perishing, but to us who are being saved it is the power of God. 1 Corinthians 1;18

It is a fact that if the Lord were to judge us according to the law none would be found worthy and we would all fall short of salvation. Knowing this and wishing that all be reconciled to himself the Lord sent his son Jesus Christ as a worthy sacrifice to earn us salvation. It is our faith in Christ that wins us the grace which earns us salvation, this faith means that we are obedient to our heavenly father and not to the flesh and its needs. It is this same faith that grants us the grace which causes us to live according to our Lord's purpose so that though we are not subject to the law we remain obedient to the Lord's word; hence we are obedient because of our faith and not obedient out of fear of judgment. Our obedience is as a result of our great love and faith in a risen Christ.

Paul's letter to the Roman's 7: 5-6, 22-25 For while we were living in the flesh, our sinful passions, aroused by the law, were at work in our members to bear fruit for death. But now we are released from the law, having died to that which held us captive, so that we may serve in the new way of the Spirit and not in the old way of the written code. For I delight in the law of God, in my inner being, but I see in my members another law waging war against the law of my mind and making me captive to the law of sin that dwells in my members. Wretched man that I am! Who will deliver me from this body of death? Thanks be to God through Jesus Christ our Lord! So then, I myself serve the law of God with my mind, but with my flesh I serve the law of sin.

This letter of Paul to the Romans is a vivid view of the struggle we experience as Christians, a war of the flesh and the Spirit. Let us remember that as Christians we have signed up to live the way of the cross. As children of God we struggle against sin, because the physical form, our flesh or human nature has a tendency to sin. If we only desire to live according to the dictates of our flesh and its needs then we cannot be obedient children of God. It is only if we are willing to struggle against the needs of the flesh that are not according to our Lord's purpose and deny ourselves, take up our cross and live according to the Spirit, that we can be true children of God. The Holy Spirit within us, which is of God abhors sin and is slave to obedience and the will of God. This is the constant struggle we encounter as children of God, the battle of the needs of the flesh against the needs of the Spirit, if we have not undergone any struggle and yet we call ourselves children of God, perhaps it is time to examine our conscience. For, the only reason we might not be struggling is because we have silenced our conscience, we have lowered our threshold; we have now justified our sinful nature and believe we have no sin. Anyone who says he has no sin is in need of an inner enlightenment. May our eyes be opened and our ears listen to the Spirit of God for it is only if we live by the Spirit that we will inherit eternal life.

Roman's 8: 17 But it is not for us to live as our human nature wants us to. For if you live according to your human nature, you are going to die but if by the Spirit you put to death your sinful actions, you will live.

As children of the flesh when faced with adversity we often grumble, much like the Israelites did when they wandered the wilderness in the time of Moses. We must learn to bear our burdens with humility even as we commit ourselves to the Lord and ask him to deliver us. We must learn to look upon our trials as a sharing in the sufferings of Christ on the cross even as our faith assures us that the Lord will deliver us from all adversity. In times of adversity let us remember to look up to the cross for it is only by death that we can be brought to rise with Christ to a new life. It is only if we look up to the cross that the adversity we conquer by the Lord's grace will bring us to a new life in the spirit as we testify of God's goodness.

Numbers 21; 4-9 From Mount Hor they set out by the way of the Red Sea, to go around the land of Edom. And the people became impatient on the way. And the people spoke against God and against Moses, "Why have you brought us up out of Egypt to die in the wilderness? For there is no food and no water, and we loathe this worthless food." Then the Lord sent fiery serpents among the people, and they bit the people, so that many people of Israel died. And the people came to Moses and said, "We have sinned, for we have spoken against the Lord and against you. Pray to the Lord, that he take away the serpents from us." So Moses prayed for the people. And the Lord said to Moses, "Make a fiery serpent and set it on a pole, and everyone who is bitten when he sees it, shall live." So Moses made a bronze serpent and set it on a pole. And if a serpent bit anyone, he would look at the bronze serpent and live.

John 3; 14-15 And as Moses lifted up the serpent in the wilderness, so must the Son of Man be lifted up, that whoever believes in him may have eternal life.

The Israelites grumbled when they were faced with adversity, they forgot how our great Lord had delivered them from the hands of the Egyptians. The serpents came and bit them even as they continued to grumble but they soon came to re-consider their actions and return in humility and true repentance as they asked Moses to pray for them and ask the Lord to take the serpents away from them. It was the Israelites who were truly repentant and had faith that the Lord would deliver them as they looked upon the bronze serpent and were saved. Those who remained filled with pride, continued to grumble and refused to have faith died in that desert at Mount Hor. Now Christ has died on the cross and rather than grumble in our adversity if we would only just lift up our eyes and gaze upon Christ on the cross. It is the faith we have that gives us the assurance that he will deliver us from our adversity and bring us to a new life in the spirit. We are all called to walk the way of the cross that brings us to a re-birth of the spirit by way of our faith. We are called to look upon Christ on the cross as the Israelites looked upon the serpent that was lifted up to them in the desert, for it is by our faith in our Christ crucified that we are granted the grace that earns us eternal life.

The Lord calls all, and the choice is ours to make freely, this is the struggle that we face as sons of God. Our vow as Christians is to forfeit the wants of the flesh where they are against the Lord's word. Each day that the Lord has given us the great gift of life, is another day of opportunity to win the battle over the wants of the flesh and live by the Spirit. Each time we face adversity and are tempted to grumble, we must remember to look upon the cross that our Lord may grant us his grace. It is by the Spirit granted us as children of God, the Spirit that causes us to be co-heirs with Christ that we win victory over the flesh. It is only in death that the battle of spirit and flesh ends. By the grace granted us on account of our faith, we can win the battle and gain victory over the flesh, but every time we lose a battle, the Lord is ever ready to console us and forgive us as he did the Israelites in the desert, even as he empowers us by his Spirit to continue to strive to win victory over the flesh.

Let us commit to remaining obedient to the Lord's will in every adversity we face especially in difficult times, just as Christ was obedient to death on the cross. Let us welcome the gift of the Holy Spirit and the grace that is ours on account of our faith and endurance as we answer the call to be co-heirs with Christ, for it is only in the Spirit that victory is possible. We must not forget in times of temptation or adversity to look upon the cross for that is where our grace was borne.

CHAPTER NINE

Obedience

And being found in human form, he humbled himself by becoming obedient to the point of death, even death on a cross. Therefore God has highly exalted him and bestowed on him the name that is above every name, so that at the name of Jesus every knee should bow, in heaven and on earth and under the earth, and every tongue confess that Jesus Christ is Lord, to the glory of God the father.

Philippians 2; 8-10

Obedience is what causes the desire for victory of the Spirit over the flesh. Our obedience is not born of fear but rather out of the great love that we have for our Lord. We desire to live according to God's precepts and be obedient to his will because we love him and want to please him. The spirit has spoken in our conscience; the way of God is made known. It is by our will that we determine to be obedient or not after we have contemplated in our hearts. For when we listen to the Holy Spirit within us and let him influence our will then we are truly sons of God, for true sons are obedient to their father.

Obedience is a virtue we must pray for as it is what causes us to choose the way of the Spirit over the way of the flesh. Obedience causes us to do as the Spirit says even when we have no idea what the consequences are of our actions. Much like a sculptor putting his hands to clay without first making a prototype of his masterpiece, obedience is a true act of faith and love. For if we obey, only then can we profess that truly we have faith in the one true God and wish to submit to him. The obedience of the children of God in this day however is freely given. Our Lord will judge us not according to the Law, but according to the love and faith we have in him. If we love God we will obey him and choose his ways over ours. Truly all are called freely to be children of God, we can all say Abba Father, if we so desire, the choice is ours. As children of God we must desire to be obedient to God's word in times of turmoil or struggle.

Much Like Abraham our father in faith was obedient to taking his son to slaughter as in Gen 22;10-13 Then Abraham reached out his hand and took the knife to slaughter his son. But the angel of the Lord called to him from heaven and said, "Abraham, Abraham" And he said, "Here I am". He said, "Do not lay your hand on the boy or do anything to him, for now I know that you fear God, seeing you have not withheld your son, your only son, from me." And Abraham lifted up his eyes and looked, and behold, behind him was a ram, caught in a thicket by his horns.

Much like Mary was obedient in conceiving of Christ in Luke 1;30, 34- 38 And the angel said to her, "Do not be afraid, Mary, for you have found favor with God. And behold you will conceive in your womb and bear a son, and you shall call his name Jesus. And Mary said to the angel, "How will this be, since I am a virgin? Behold, I am the servant of the Lord; let it be done to me according to your word"

Mary was in a state of turmoil as she pondered in her heart how she, an unmarried virgin was to conceive of a child, in a day and age where this was unacceptable. Was she to be the talk of the town, jeered at, ridiculed, possibly stoned to death. Mary did not weaken in her turmoil and say no, her will was subject to the Holy Spirit not her flesh and she did what was right in the eyes of God by saying these fulfilling words. Mary's total yes to our Lord with no reservation, shows her perfect submission, she overcame her doubt and fear and was obedient even when she knew not how it would turn out, her obedience showed that she had great faith and love for our Lord.

Much like Christ was obedient to his father throughout his lifetime on earth. Christ shows us the greatest demonstration of obedience to his Father by his crucifixion on the cross through which he gave us the ultimate gift - his life. Christ was indeed in a state of struggle, when he said during his crucifixion, Matthew 27: 46 "My God, my God why have you forsaken me" but he did not allow his flesh to overcome the spirit nature within him. He warred and he battled and by his will he was obedient to his father, even to death on the cross. Even as we mocked him, spat at him and jeered at him, he said these redeeming words, Luke 23: 34 "Father, forgive them for they know not what they do". The Lord is even more pleased when we obey him in difficult times, when we choose the way of the spirit over the way that our human flesh desires. Obedience of the children of God is as a consequence of the true love and faith we have in our Lord. Christ was obedient at that final moment of his death as he gave up his Spirit in Luke 23;46 Then Jesus calling out with a loud voice said, "Father into your hands I commit my spirit!" And having said this he breathed his last.

We cannot be children of the Spirit if we are not obedient as Christ was, and if we say we have a true love and faith in our Lord yet fail to be obedient to his word then we are nothing less than hypocrites. May our love and faith in the one true Lord bring us to a life of obedience to his Spirit for true obedience is synonymous with faith.

CHAPTER TEN

Free Will

Christ's words at the agony in the Garden of Gethsemane on the Mount of Olives are another true demonstration of total submission to God's will and true obedience in Luke 22; 42"Father if you are willing, remove this cup from me. Nevertheless, not my will, but yours be done".

Even when Christ was apprehensive of the trials to come he remained ready to submit to his father's will. We all know how difficult it is to defer to the will of another more especially if it would cause us to suffer. Each time we are hesitant to act in keeping with the Lord's will, let us remember that it was Christ's crucifixion that earned us our salvation and that whatever trials we undergo as long as we remain in a state of total submission to the Lord's will, the outcome will bring us victory in the Spirit.

During 'The Agony in the Garden of Gethsemane', the reality of the suffering Christ was to experience was fully revealed to him. Christ could have chosen not to drink of the cup of his crucifixion by his own free will, but rather he chose to be obedient to his father and gained victory of the Spirit over the flesh. After Christ consented to God's will an angel appeared to him and strengthened him, if we choose to do God's will and subject our spirit to his Spirit, he will send us his grace and strengthen us by and his angels, he never leaves his children to suffer alone. It was out of God's love for us that he gave us the gift of free will. In times of temptation, we go to war with our conscience, the spirit form within us wars with our human nature or flesh. The mere fact that we are in a state of struggle means that our Spirit form in our conscience has judged us and made it clear to us that it is a temptation that might cause us to fall out of grace that we face. It is now up to the spirit form in our will to make a decision; consent or not to consent to overcome the struggle that the Lord has allowed us to experience. Light will always conquer darkness, good always conquers evil so the spirit will always conquer the flesh if we allow it, and victory is always ours for the taking. By the gift of free will the Lord has given us a choice, it becomes our decision to make; do we desire to win or give up the battle. The Lord has given us the Holy Spirit living within us in our conscience to help us, guide us, instruct us and teach us. Yet despite knowing the right way we very often quiet the spirit within us by justifying our actions, repeatedly indulging the flesh and refusing to overcome the struggle, and eventually we harden our hearts and cause the Holy Spirit within us to depart. At any point in time where we encounter a struggle we must turn to the Spirit form within us and communicate with the Lord in Prayer and supplication, much like Christ did when he experienced the agony in the garden. It becomes a battle of Spirit and flesh, for the flesh often would rather fall into temptation and experience the pleasure that fulfilling the needs of the flesh brings, but the Spirit seeks to be obedient to our Lord's will and fulfill his commands. By ourselves alone it is tough to win a struggle but by the grace of the Holy Spirit within us, we can overcome our struggles and remain obedient to God's will. Let not forget that for any one of us undergoing a form of struggle we are not alone, as brothers and sisters we are one in the spirit and we must pray together that the Lord will strengthen us by his Spirit.

Let us not take it for granted that Christ was crucified for our salvation. Let us not assume that it so happened because it was pre-destined. Christ was made to be man, so that he also was of flesh and Spirit as we are. The narration of the agony in the Garden makes it clear that Christ was as much flesh as he was Spirit. It was clearly a time of struggle for Christ, a time when he could have by his own free will decided not to offer himself as a living sacrifice after he experienced a preview of his crucifixion exactly as it was to occur. Christ knew his time had come, he actually experienced a glimpse of what he was to experience on the cross, so that he was well informed, and he could then truly make an informed decision to consent or not to consent to his crucifixion. Note that as soon as Christ consented to his father's will his anguish did not cease, for he still perspired sweat that was like blood. This experience was intense and vivid, despite this Christ did not give in. We must learn that true obedience to God means surrendering to his will especially in difficult times. We do not surrender out of fear but on account of our faith; much like Christ did, knowing that our destiny can only be fulfilled in as much as we surrender to the Holy Spirit and allow him to direct our actions. If we act according to the Spirit in all situations, only then can we experience the eternal life that we are promised as God's children. Our Lord offers his grace to us all freely to enable us achieve this ultimate goal for which we daily strive, to gain victory of the spirit over the flesh. Sins of the flesh are deadly because they separate us from God. Once we give up the fight and give in, once we stop running the race and struggling, by our own free will we have chosen death over life, flesh over spirit. The choice is always ours to make and as children of God we must choose the way of the Spirit over the way of the flesh as Christ did, by our own free will knowing that God's grace is sufficient to grant us victory in all battles we may face.

True faith in Christ means we die to the flesh and willingly let the Spirit lead us. To die to the flesh and rise to a new life in the Spirit requires a faith that is synonymous with total submission but as people of flesh the concept of total submission is difficult to conceive. If we believe we must submit in true faith as we say the words of Our Father's prayer, "Thy will be done".

Galatians 2:20 I have been crucified with Christ. It is no longer I who live, but Christ who lives in me. And the life I now live in the flesh I live by faith in the son of God, who loved me and gave himself for me.

CHAPTER ELEVEN

God's Love

John 3; 16 -17 For God so loved the world that he gave his one and only Son, that whoever believes in him shall not perish but have eternal life. For God did not send his son into the world to condemn the world, but in order that the world might be saved through him.

We must understand God's love before we can even attempt to begin to share a message of 'obedience'.

Love is a verb, a doing word, an action word, not just an emotion or a feeling we feel. Love is active in our daily lives. Just as all energy flows from the sun, so also all love flows from God. The Lord is the source of all love. God's love is present from the beginning of time, the time of creation. It is out of love, that our Lord created us as man. Perhaps he had a little selfish intent when he created us out of love, for us to love him back in return. Note the word 'return' for our Lord has loved us first and is not asking us of anything less than he has first asked himself. It is out of love that the Lord also gives us free will, because our love is genuine only if it is offered freely.

The word of God defines love in 1 Corinthians 13: 4 - "Love is patient, love is kind. It does not envy, it does not boast, it is not proud. It does not insist on its own way, it is not irritable or resentful; it does not rejoice at wrongdoing but rejoices with the truth. Love bears all things, believes all things, hopes all things, and endures all things".

As children of God it is the love we have for our Lord and for each other that should cause us to stand out and shine, as we reflect God's glory. Christ loved us so much that he made restitution for all of our sin by his death, the lamb was slain once, and we will never need to offer another living sacrifice because he was slain once and for us all. Hence we should be prepared to offer all we have and are, even unto our death. Our own death is not necessary to earn salvation for mankind, but we must die to the desires of our flesh daily and submit to the will of the Spirit to inherit God's kingdom. This is how much our hearts should burn with love for Christ, much like a mother's love for her son, so our Love for Christ should be a love that is not at all selfish, but rather selfless, giving ourselves up to God's Glory. The greatest evidence of God's love for us is that despite our sinful nature and a lack of obedience to his word, he repeatedly has tried to draw us back to himself up until he gave up his only begotten son that we may have life within us. Our Lord is not pleased to see his creation live subject to the flesh rather than subject to the Spirit. His sole purpose is that we return to him at the end of time hence he takes no pleasure in our worldliness or lack of obedience that will lead us to death. This is the reason that he sent us his only begotten son, to restore to us the glory of being called sons of God. Not adopted sons, but biological sons, our DNA must have the spirit portion coded by the Holy Spirit because we are born of him.

Just as our first father Adam sinned and separated us from the love of God, so Christ came to restore us to God's love. Moses attempted this by bringing us the law, but our sinful nature meant that we could not earn salvation by obedience to the law. Our sinful nature was not capable of complete obedience to God's law. Abraham our father in faith came and showed us the meaning of true obedience, he believed and obeyed even when he knew not how God's word would come to fulfillment. His faith was the only guarantee he had, that God's word would be fulfilled. Abraham's great faith must have been a result of the great love he had for our Lord, for there can be no faith if we do not first have love. This same faith we have in a risen Christ has earned us eternal life not by obedience to the law but because of the grace earned us by Christ when he died for us on the cross. It is only because we believe (have faith) that Christ died as the final sacrifice for our sinful nature to be restored to God's glory, that we have been given the grace. This grace has earned us our salvation and gives us a new birth-right to eternal life. This is how much God loves us, our Lord loves us so much that he refuses to allow us to be separated from him, he wishes for us to share eternal life with him at the end of time, all he asks is that we have faith, this is how much he loves us.

So now that we understand a little bit of how much God loves us maybe we can even begin to understand what it means to love our Lord. Our love for Christ means this; that we have given up our sinful selves, that we have carried the cross of burdens that lay in the path of our salvation, that because of our love for God, we have chosen the spirit over the flesh and we will live a life of struggle till the last day. Our love for God means that we give up the flesh and its selfish needs and strive to be obedient to God's word, because we know that we are assured on account of our faith of the grace that earns us a guaranteed welcome to God's eternal kingdom. The love we have for our Heavenly Father is what keeps us in the race, we never stop running, we never give up, we remain obedient till the last day, because the prize is ours to take at the finish line, the prize of eternal life.

John 6; 37-40 All that the Father gives me will come to me, and whoever comes to me I will never cast out. For I have come down from heaven, not to do my own will but the will of him who sent me. And this is the will of him who sent me, that I should lose nothing of all that he has given me, but raise it up on the last day. For this is the will of my Father, that everyone who looks on the son and believes in him should have eternal life, and I will raise him up on the last day.

This great love we have for our Lord causes us to worship him, adore him, glorify him, and serve him. Even as we cry out to our Lord in prayer and supplication we must always remember to give him the glory in worship because he is the source of all we have and are that is good. The love we have for our Lord must cause us to see him in the hearts of others around us for he dwells in each of us, the love of God that flows to us must flow out and be shared with our neighbors. We often have lofty dreams of changing the world with God's love and this can only start if we share it with those around us that are in need of help. As much as we see the glory of Christ in our strength, perseverance and endurance we must also remember to see the face of Christ in the weakness of those in need, the orphans and widows, the sick, the hungry, the homeless, those suffering from addiction or any affliction, those who are so consumed by the needs of their flesh that they have lost the place in their heart that gives God the glory for all things. As much as we love our Lord and love our families, we must share our love by allowing ourselves be moved to compassion as we reach out to others. Each time we feed the hungry, give drink to the thirsty, shelter the homeless, clothe the naked, visit the sick and those imprisoned we are reaching out to love our neighbor. As we reach out to widows and orphans in need of help to empower them to obtain an education and be self-sufficient, we are truly doing God's work. As we provide for the needs of the flesh out of love, we must not forget to provide for the needs of the spirit; we must pray for one another, forgive one another when we offend each other, comfort the sorrowful, share the word with unbelievers, correct sinners using God's word, share the word with those in doubt and bear wrongs patiently, a true child of God is slow to use his tongue in anger but always reaches out in love. Our prayer is that the Lord will minister to unbelievers by our love and this love will bring them to a new life in the Spirit. Our Lord never failed to see the needs of the crowd and feed the flesh, even as much as he continued to feed the spirit with his word. Our physical needs can stand in the way of our spiritual needs because if you are consumed with hunger your priority becomes finding food and not sharing God's word or doing his work, as we feed the flesh out of love for our neighbor, let us not forget to feed the spirit also lest our work be in vain.

Each time we attend church, we are well dressed and sit in pews lined with believers who have come to hear God's word, we must stop a minute and ask ourselves even as we sit, where are the unbelievers? For our Lord to transform the world we must present ourselves before him, the great love we have for God must cause us to reach out to non-believers that we may present them all before him as his sheep. We must not provide for the needy to satisfy our own selfish needs, we must provide for them so that the Spirit of

God can minister to them and transform them, this is how our love for God and love for our neighbor will transform the world.

CHAPTER TWELVE

Repentance and Reconciliation

Luke 15; 4-7, 8-10, 17-20, 22-24

"What man of you, having a hundred sheep, if he has lost one of them, does not leave the ninety-nine in the open country and go after the one that is lost, until he finds it? And when he has found it, he lays it on his shoulder rejoicing. And when he comes home, he calls his friends and neighbors, saying to them, 'Rejoice with me, for I have found my sheep that was lost.' Just so, I tell you, there will be more joy in heaven over one sinner who repents than over ninety-nine righteous persons who need no repentance.

Or what woman, having ten silver coins, if she loses one coin, does not light a lamp and sweep the house and seek diligently until she finds it? And when she has found it, she calls together her friends and neighbor, saying, 'Rejoice with me, for I have found the coin that I had lost.' Just so, I tell you, there is joy before the angels of God over one sinner who repents."

"But when he came to himself, he said how many of my father's hired servants have more than enough bread, but I perish here with hunger! I will arise and go to my father, and I will say to him, "Father, I have sinned against heaven and before you. I am no longer worthy to be called your son. Treat me as one of your hired servants. And he arose and came to his father .But the father said to his servants, 'Bring quickly the best robe and put it on him, and put a ring on his hand, and shoes on his feet. And bring the fattened calf and kill it, and let us eat and celebrate. For this my son was dead and is alive again; he was lost and is found.' And they began to celebrate.

Each souls that is lost wandering is precious to our Lord despite the many that have come back home to him. Each believer that is yet to claim his salvation is worth much to Christ despite the many that have claimed the salvation that is ours on account of our faith in a risen Christ. This is why Jesus Christ is the good Shepherd for he does not wish to loose even one sheep of his fold, his heart is heavy and weary when a single of his sheep wanders away or is lost. The Lord wishes that each of us like the prodigal son arise from our life of sin and debauchery and return to a life of the Spirit. Our Lord Jesus Christ gave his life on the cross for our salvation, yet man that he made this ultimate sacrifice for continues to live in sin and refuses to repent and return to him our Father. Jesus is alive yesterday, as he is today and will be forever, he came to this world to earn us salvation. By the ultimate act of his crucifixion we gained salvation. Christ continues to experience sorrow as he watches upon the world and we refuse to repent and return to him as we are too busy living. Despite Christ's ultimate sacrifice of giving up his own life and making salvation attainable to all, man continues to choose to indulge the selfish needs of the flesh over the spirit and repeatedly rejects the free gift of salvation. Christ is filled with sorrow because we repeatedly refuse his offer of eternal paradise and everlasting life when we refuse his grace that he gives freely to earn us salvation. The grace we earned through no effort save our faith and solely by his death on the cross. We earned salvation not by obedience to the Law, but through Christ's eternal sacrifice, freely given at no cost, save that we believe. It is the faith we lack that causes us to question Christ's love for us, to doubt the truth that is our salvation and that should bring us to true repentance. Surely, if we truly believe in a risen Christ, we must arise like the prodigal son and return to the house of our Father. We must repent and not allow the selfish desires of the flesh separate us from the love of Christ.

Roman's 3:23 But now the righteousness of God has been manifested apart from the law, although the Law and the Prophets bear witness to it – the righteousness of God through faith in Jesus Christ for all who believe. For there is no distinction; for all have sinned and fall short of the glory of God and are justified by his grace as a gift, through the redemption that is in Christ Jesus, whom God put forward as a holy sacrifice by shedding his blood, to be received by faith.

We have all sinned and fallen short of God's glory, but all hope is not lost. Let us liken a man living in sin to the prodigal son, and say, 'I have voluntarily removed myself from my father's house. I have gone wandering in the desert of life, and squandered my inheritance. But as long as I have life, I have hope, for there is a chance of repentance,' therefore life is one of the greatest gifts the Lord can give us. Though we have lost all things, if we have life it is for a reason, so that we may have an opportunity for repentance. Christ is waiting for us to return to him, much like the ninety-nine sheep the shepherd left at home, to rescue the one. Much like the nine coins the widow left, to find the one. Much like the prodigal son whose father awaited his return, our Lord is awaiting our return. Our heavenly father eagerly awaits our arrival, for we are part of his body, if we are in pain, he feels our pain, if we are separated from him his joy is not complete. The Lord awaits our return, so that we may be restored to him and his joy may be complete. It is by our will that the decision must be made by each of us. Much like the prodigal son awoke from his slumber and realized he really had no reason to live a life of wretchedness; all he had to do was get up, and go home. So it is with us all that live in sin, it is time to awaken from our slumber, get up and go home. The time to say no to our flesh, and yes to Christ and obedience, the time to die to our flesh with its needs, and rise to our Spirit and God's word is now. There is much rejoicing in heaven as we die to our flesh and rise to a new life in the spirit. This re-birth causes the heavenly host to sing and rejoice; for each lost son that is returned, there is much rejoicing in heaven. Likewise Christ is filled with sorrow each time we say yes to our flesh and its sinful needs, and we say no to Christ and a way that is righteous. Each time by our own free will we decide to take up our armor, breast plate and shield and decide to return to the war as children of the Lord, a fattened calf is killed and a heavenly choir of angels sings out. It is time we caused the heavenly host to sing a resounding chorus of Alleluia.

Christ on the cross asks us this one question; 'If you were without sin and righteous why would I have had to give up my life for you?' For those of us who are without sin and righteous, we have no need of Christ crucified. It is precisely for those of us in a state of sin that Christ had to be crucified, as he came not for the righteous but for sinners. Our Lord's will is that all sinners repent and re-unite with him now and at the end of time. It is for those who thirst that Christ comes to offer to drink of the living waters of our salvation, to those who hunger he comes to offer the living bread of his flesh, to those who are lost he has come to find them and those who seek salvation he has brought fulfillment. Christ tells us the story of the widow, the shepherd and the prodigal son to illustrate that he is ever willing to re-unite us to himself if we so desire. We in turn must repent, give up the needs of our flesh that are against Christ's will, and surrender to him.

CHAPTER THIRTEEN

God's Mercy

1 John 1:9 If we confess our sins, he is faithful and just to forgive us our sins and to cleanse us from all unrighteousness.

Christ is indeed the good shepherd, he knows his sheep and we his sheep know him. He wishes that not even one of his sheep is lost. He known no rest until every single one of his sheep is returned. He knows us each by name and calls us one by one. All that is required is that we answer 'I will' and indeed there is much rejoicing in heaven as each and every one of us answer the call to salvation and allow the Holy Spirit to transform us.

The only thing that can separate us from God's mercy is our own flesh, by our free will. Since we have all sinned and know that we have fallen short of God's glory, why are we not all repentant, confessing our sins and asking for forgiveness? Christ on the cross with open arms continues to weep as tears of blood when we make it seem that his death was in vain. For his crucifixion was of no value to us if we continue to live in sin and refuse to repent. As we are busy pursuing our daily lives, we appear to be in a state of constant daily activity, this daily activity while necessary for many of us to earn a living can also cause us to live a facade. We are so busy with the activity of our daily lives that we fail to take a minute to examine our conscience and listen to the Spirit within us speak. We must take the time to retreat from our lives on a daily basis and find time to meditate on God's word and listen to our conscience. The Lord will speak to us in our Spirit and correct us on the error of our ways, he will enlighten us of our shortcomings and open our eyes to our sinfulness. It is only after such inner reflection, retreat or meditation that we can confess our sins, repent and ask for forgiveness. Catholics offer the sacrament of confession where each individual has the opportunity to examine their conscience, confess their sin and ask the Lord for forgiveness, the Priest as Christ's Apostle absolves each repentant sinner and asks them to go and sin no more. Other Christian denominations confess their sins to the Lord in prayer as they repent and ask the Lord for forgiveness. Whichever belief we have as Christians, we must retreat from our daily activities examine our conscience, confess our sin, repent and receive the Lord's forgiveness with true contrition.

John 20;21-23 Jesus said to them again, "Peace be with you. As the Father has sent me so I am sending you." And when he had said this, he breathed on them and said to them, "Receive the Holy Spirit. If you forgive the sins of any, they are forgiven them; if you withhold forgiveness from any, it is withheld."

We should take it upon ourselves as Christians on a regular basis to examine our conscience, repent and ask for forgiveness from our Lord with a true and contrite heart. We must not allow the business and activity of our daily lives, sin, shame denial or our own justification of our actions cause us to justify our sin and excuse our bad behavior. Each time we return to Christ to be forgiven and re-united with him in true contrition he is indeed pleased and ever ready to forgive each and every one of us. We must not allow ourselves to be separated from Christ's mercy because we fail to present ourselves to him and allow him to absolve us from our sin. True faith means that we do not question the Lord's mercy and his ever being ready to forgive our sin. As we receive forgiveness of sin from our Lord, we also must remember to forgive one another even as we strive not to sin again. If we are truly contrite of our own sin, we must not help but be willing to forgive those who have offended us and then we can truly say we have come full circle. It is only if we allow the Holy Spirit to transform our hearts that we can let go of the pride that stands in the way of our reconciliation with Christ and with our neighbor.

Matthew 6;14-15 For if you forgive others their trespasses, your heavenly Father will also forgive you, but if you do not forgive others their trespasses, neither will your Father forgive your trespasses.

CHAPTER FOURTEEN

God's Word

2Timothy 3; 16-17 All scripture is breathed out by God and profitable for teaching, for reproof, for correction, and for training in righteousness, that the man of God may be complete, equipped for every good work.

The word of God is Spirit because it has life in the form of a cause and effect nature to it. The word has the power to convert us in the Spirit. It is through Christ's word that the message of salvation is passed on from generation to generation. Much like bread is food for the body, so the word is food for the Spirit. The word confirms the will of the Lord for us all. It explains the purpose for which we are created then teaches and explains what is required of us as children of God. The word also causes us to know what is right in the sight of our Lord. It is a measure by which we can judge our thoughts and actions, much like our conscience, the word can correct us, implore us, inspire us, alert us, motivate us, and the word is Spirit, which is the Holy Spirit speaking to us and can convert us. This is why we must meditate on the word, evangelize with the word, share the word and allow the word to convert us so that we return as sheep to the good Shepherd who is Jesus Christ.

Hebrews 4:12 For the word of God is living and active, sharper than any two-edged sword, piercing to the division of soul and of spirit, of joints and of marrow, and discerning the thoughts and intentions of the heart. And no creature is hidden from his sight, but all are naked and exposed to the eyes of him to whom we must give account.

The only way to allow the word of God which is Christ himself transform us is to speak it, share it, profess it, study it, meditate on it and apply it to our daily lives. The word will feed our spirit, nurture our conscience, instruct us in the way of true obedience, reprimand us, correct us, inspire us and strengthen us in the Spirit, for it has the power to do so. As Christians we often become complacent in our duty of studying and sharing the word. We leave it to our Pastors, Priests and Preachers to study the word and share it with us. As children it is appropriate that we be guided and led by our spiritual leaders, however at a certain point in our Spiritual life we must reach the maturity where we take up the baton after we have been schooled. We also must study and share the word and this is why the word never is dormant because after it transforms us, we transform others by sharing, and this is how the work of evangelization continues. The word has existed since before the beginning of creation and as long as we continue to do as Christ instructed, the word will continue to exist until the end of time. All Christians should have sisters and brothers in faith with whom they share and study the word, it is our duty as Christians, we must limit no one from our sharing and we must call upon the Spirit to lead us and guide us each time we share the word.

John 6: 63 It is the Spirit who gives life; the flesh is no help at all. The words that I have spoken with you are spirit and life.

As long as we allow the word of God to transform us in our spirit we will indeed receive a re-birth to new life in obedience and love of our Lord.

The word of God existed from the beginning of time and is the source of all creation. We can therefore comprehend that the word of God is Spirit, if we understand how our Lord created the world by speaking the word. We can also appreciate how the word is God himself in the Spirit for what you believe is what you speak and what you speak defines you for who you are. As man it is the words we speak that represent our very selves. Christ is his word, for his very essence is contained within it. We can also see how Christ himself who is one with his Father existed in spirit form in the word at the beginning of all creation. We must never underestimate the power of the word as it is spirit, which is why it had power to create the world, why it can transform us and convert us and why we must speak it in the spirit of faith, resting assured in the true confidence that that the word can create, transform and change.

John 1: 1: In the beginning was the Word, and the Word was with God, and the Word was God

CHAPTER FIFTEEN

The Body and Blood of Christ

Christ offered up his body and blood unto us as bread and wine and asked us to continue this practice in memory of him. Luke 22;19 And he took bread, and when he had given thanks, he broke it and gave it to them, saying, "This is my body, which is given for you. Do this in remembrance of me".

Just as bread and wine are food for the body, so the body and blood of Christ is food for our spirit and soul. We must nourish our spirit with the word as well as with the body and blood of Christ. Christ in the form of his body and blood provides us with the inner strength and the grace to be true children of God. Just as the word can convert us in Spirit, so the body and blood of Christ can covert us and renew us in the Spirit. Various Christian denominations have varying doctrine on the body and blood of Christ but all generally agree that the body and blood of Christ in the form of bread and wine offered as Holy Communion by an anointed Pastor or Priest is nourishment for the spirit and welcomes Christ to reside in us as his holy Temple. Unfortunately, often, as Christians of modern times as these we choose to believe in only what can be proven by science, however mysteries of the Spirit cannot be proven by science, it is with faith that we believe, with the hope that all mysteries of God's kingdom will be revealed to us at the end of time. This is why we must be like little children to enter God's kingdom, it is our faith that causes us to be like little children, because we believe in God's word even when it cannot be scientifically proven. If we believe that Bread gives food to the flesh, then we must also believe that Christ is bread for the Spirit. Just as the flesh cannot be sustained without bread or food, so also we ourselves as Christians cannot be sustained in our spirit without feeding it with the Bread of life, which is Christ himself. We must receive Christ as the true bread that gives life to our Spirit.

John 6; 48 – 51 I am the bread of life. Your fathers ate the manna in the wilderness and they died. This is the bread that comes down from heaven, so that one may eat of it and not die. I am the living bread that came down from heaven. If anyone eats of this bread, he will live forever. And the bread that I will give for the life of the world is my flesh." The Jews then disputed among themselves saying, "How can this man give us his flesh to eat?" So Jesus said to them, "Truly, truly, I say to you, unless you eat the flesh of the son of Man and drink his blood, you have no life in you. Whoever feeds on my flesh and drinks my blood has eternal life, and I will raise him up on the last day. For my flesh is true food, and my blood is true drink. Whoever feeds on my flesh and drinks my blood abides in me, and I in him. As the living Father sent me, and I live because of the Father, so whoever feeds on me, he also will live because of me. This is the bread that came down from heaven, not like the bread your fathers ate, and died. Whoever feeds on this bread will live forever."

After these words of Christ, his disciples were confused and many of his followers departed. Perhaps they could not understand how Christ was to be their bread and how they were to consume him so that he may reside within them and grant them eternal life. Our faith as children of God means that we believe each and every word Christ tells us. Our faith should cause us to know that Christ truly dwells within the form of bread and wine as his body and blood. It is impressionable that Christ did not call back the followers that walked away at his proclamation as 'the body and blood that gives life.' The faith that we have as children of the Lord causes us to hope that at the end of time all God's children will be returned to him, and for those times when we question Christ's word we pray for the gift of faith and the grace that it brings.

For us to begin to understand how we can eat the bread that is Christ's flesh and the wine that is his blood we must first refer to the Old Testament for a short while.

Exodus 12: 5-7,29: Your lamb shall be without blemish, a male, a year old. You may take it from the sheep or from the goats, and you shall keep it until the fourteenth day of this month, when the whole assembly of the congregation of Israel shall kill their lambs at twilight." Then they shall take some of the blood and put it on the two doorposts and the lintel of the houses in which they eat it .In this manner you shall eat it with your belt fastened, your sandals on your feet, and your staff in your hand. And you shall eat it in haste, it is the Lord's Passover. For I will pass through the land of Egypt that night, and I will strike all the first born in the land of Egypt, both man and beast; and on all the Gods of Egypt I will execute judgments; I am the Lord. The blood shall be a sign for you, on the houses where you are. And when I see the blood, I will pass over you, and no plague will befall you to destroy you, when I strike the land of Egypt. "This day shall be for you a memorial day, and you shall keep it as a feast to the Lord; throughout your generations, as a statute forever, you shall keep it as a feast. At midnight the Lord struck down all the firstborn of the land of Egypt, from the first born of Pharaoh who sat on the throne, to the firstborn of the captive who was in the dungeon, and all the firstborn of the livestock.

We can see how the Israelites were delivered by our Lord from the hand of the Egyptians, the blood of the Lamb that they had slain delivered them from all evil, as evil passed over them on that fateful day of the Passover. If the blood of the lamb that was slain was able to deliver the Israelites from the evil that was to befall the Egyptians, how much more will the blood of the true Lamb Jesus Christ that was shed for us at Christ's crucifixion deliver us from the evil of sin and death, and earn us the grace that brings salvation to the children of God. We must also note how The Lord instructed that the Israelites were to keep the Passover as a memorial day, in the same was Christ whose blood was to serve as the new Passover asks that we give thanks and break bread in memory of him.

Exodus 16;2-5,14-15, 19-20 And the whole congregation of the people of Israel grumbled against Moses and Aaron in the wilderness, and the people of Israel said to them, "Would that we had died by the hand of the Lord in the land of Egypt, when we sat by the meat pots and ate bread to the full, for you have brought us into this wilderness to kill this whole assembly with hunger." Then the Lord said to Moses, "Behold, I am about to rain bread from heaven for you, and the people shall go out and gather a day's portion every day, that I may test them, whether they will walk in my law or not. On the sixth day, when they prepare what they bring in, it will be twice as much as they gather daily." And when the dew had gone up, there was on the face of the wilderness a fine, flake-like thing, fine as frost on the ground. When the people of Israel saw it they, they said to one another, "What is it?" for they did not know what it was. And Moses said to them, "It is the bread that the Lord has given you to eat". And Moses said to them, "Let no one leave any of it over till the morning." But they did not listen to Moses. Some left part of it till the morning, and it bred worms and stank. And Moses was angry with them

The Israelites after haven been delivered from the hands of the Egyptians grumbled and complained when it appeared to them as if the Lord had deserted them in the desolate land of the desert. They quickly forgot the great evil from which the Lord had delivered them in the hands of the Egyptians, but the Lord listened to their complaints and gave them bread from heaven as food, this bread was not everlasting, it would go bad after a certain period, this bread did not bring the Israelites everlasting life, they would die after a time. Jesus Christ came and offered himself as the bread that was everlasting, if we eat of him we would never hunger, for he would forever feed our Spirit, nurture our Spirit and strengthen it, we would never die for if we eat of him we would be as him, forever obedient to the will of his father and faithful to his call, as we receive Christ into our hearts with true faith he grants us the grace that is indeed sufficient to earn us eternal life all we have to do is taste and see. Unfortunately despite our Lord trying again and again to reconcile us to himself we continue to be disobedient as the Israelites were when they tried to preserve their manna, we continue to fail to have a true faith that causes us to be obedient to God's word, the time for reconciliation is now.

John 6: 56-57 Whoever feeds on my flesh and drinks my blood abides in me, and I in him. As the living father sent me, and I live because of the Father, so whoever feeds on me, he also will live because of me.

CHAPTER SIXTEEN

Faith and God's Grace

Ephesians 2; 8-10 For by grace you have been saved through faith. And this is not your own doing; it is the gift of God, not a result of works, so that no one may boast. For we are his workmanship, created in Christ Jesus for good works, which God prepared beforehand, that we should walk in them.

The greatest gift available to us that earns us eternal life is our faith, after Christ was crucified on the cross we received the gift of our salvation on account of our faith. Christ by the great sacrifice of his crucifixion put us in the right with our Lord. If we believe that sin came into the world through one man Adam, and that this sin of disobedience leads us to death, then we must also believe that through this one righteous man; Christ and his one righteous act; his crucifixion in obedience, he earned us our salvation. Can we say that because we have received the gift of salvation through Christ's sacrifice on the cross that we are no longer subject to the Law? True, indeed, we are no longer subject to the law, because it is our faith in Christ, not obedience to the law that has earned us righteousness. This does not mean that the law does not exist, or that we should allow the flesh victory over the Spirit. This simply means that, as long we have faith in a risen Christ, we have been put right with our Lord. The question then becomes what is this faith that we have in a risen Lord? Our faith is our belief in Jesus Christ our Lord, that he was born into this world to earn our salvation, that he was crucified on the cross for our sake, died and resurrected from the dead on the third day, that he ascended into heaven where he sits at our Lord's right hand. This faith in a risen Lord means that we are obedient to his word, faith is therefore synonymous with obedience and righteousness, much like our Father Abraham, our mother Mary and Christ Jesus our savior were obedient to God's word and were righteous in God's sight. As long as we have a faith in the risen Christ there is no question that he will grant us the grace to live in obedience to his word.

What is this grace that we have earned by our faith? Grace is the Spirit of Christ that dwells within us, that speaks to us in God's word and strengthens us by our will to remain obedient to our Lord. Our faith causes us to give up the flesh as we are no longer subject to its needs, as we die to the flesh it is the grace of the Holy Spirit that causes us to rise in the spirit of Christ. It is this grace we have been granted on account of our faith that causes our spirit to win victory over the flesh.

Romans 4;16 That is why it depends on faith, in order that the promise may rest on grace and be guaranteed to all his offspring – not only to the adherent of the law but also to the one who shares the faith of Abraham, who is the father of us all.

Romans 5 1-5,17,20,21- "Therefore, since we have been justified by faith, we have peace with God through our Lord Jesus Christ.

Through him we have also received access by faith into this grace in which we stand, and we rejoice in hope of the glory of God. Not only that, but we rejoice in our sufferings, knowing that suffering produces endurance, and endurance produces character and character produces hope, and hope does not put us to shame, because God's love has been poured into our hearts through the Holy spirit who has been given to us. For if because of one man's trespass, death reigned through that one man, much more will those who receive the abundance of grace and the free gift of righteousness reign in life through the one man Jesus Christ. Now the law came in to increase the trespass, but where sin increased, grace abounded all the more, so that as sin reigned in death, grace also might reign through righteousness leading to eternal life through Jesus Christ our Lord".

As much as our faith earns us the grace to be children of God that are obedient and righteous we must never cease from prayer. At all times, prayer must remain our mode of communication with our Lord, we must call on him in our time of need, receive his body and blood humbly and share his word as these are the tools that aid us in our struggle to earn eternal life.

Romans 6; 9-14 We know that Christ, being raised from the dead, will never die again; death no longer has dominion over him. For the death he died he died to sin, once for all, but the life he lives he lives to God. So you also must consider yourselves dead to sin and alive to God in Christ Jesus. Let not sin therefore reign in your mortal body, to make you obey its passions. Do not present your members to sin as instruments of unrighteousness, but present yourselves to God as instruments for righteousness. For sin will have no dominion over you, since you are not under the law but under God's grace.

So who is worthy of salvation, who is worthy to be called sons of God, who are God's chosen people?

All are called, and all are welcome, this is specifically why Christ gave of himself freely, as a holy sacrifice on the cross, that all might receive salvation. Our Lord loved us completely from the time he created us, it is out of this love for us that he made us to be like him and gave us a purpose and free will. He wishes that we love him in return, love each other and freely do his will. When Christ died on the cross, his greatest desire was that every one of us should receive the salvation his death earned us. This is why Christ calls each of us to die with him to sin and the flesh by our baptism and rise to a new life in the Spirit as he rose to a new life by his resurrection. This is why sin has no power over us, because the flesh has no power over the Holy Spirit that dwells within us. We are no longer slaves of sin that leads to death, instead we are slaves to obedience which leads to righteousness and everlasting life in the Spirit. It is the Spirit of Christ that dwells within us and gives us the grace of victory over the flesh. This is the grace Christ earned for us by his death on the cross; his Spirit within us to convert us from within and empower us as we strive to be obedient sons to our father. This is the grace that we have received by virtue of our faith; simply because we believe. Whether Jew or Gentile, rich or poor man, slave or freeman, able or disabled if we believe in our hearts and we profess by our mouth a faith in Christ the risen Lord, this grace is ours. It is this grace of the Holy Spirit within us that we have freely received by virtue of our faith that brings us to be obedient to our Father as Christ himself was obedient. It is our faith that causes us to be slaves to obedience and righteousness, rather than slaves to the flesh and sinfulness.

It is unfortunately true that, many have eyes and refuse to see, ears and refuse to hear, and they have hardened their hearts, it is to these lost souls that we belong if we turn our backs on the free gift of our salvation. We must not turn our backs on Christ as he gives up his life on the cross and died once and for all to sin, rather we must unite ourselves with Christ as we die to our flesh so that we may all rise with him in the Spirit, to inherit everlasting life.

In Paul's letter to the Ephesians he warns us about the temptations we must overcome, the essential armor we require shielding us, and strengthening us as we fight to win victory of the spirit over the flesh. Let us never forget that we are children of the light and that darkness has no part in us, we must continue to reflect the light of our almighty Lord. As soldiers called to the army, we must go into the battle of life with the necessary armor to win victory over the flesh.

Ephesians 6: 10 - 20 "Finally, be strong in the Lord and in the strength of his might. Put on the whole armor of God, that you may be able to stand against the schemes of the devil. For we do not wrestle against flesh and blood, but against the rulers, against the authorities, against the cosmic powers over this present darkness, against the spiritual forces of evil in the heavenly places. Therefore take up the whole armor of God, that you may be able to withstand in the evil day, and having done all, to stand firm. Stand therefore having fastened on the belt of truth, and having put on the breastplate of righteousness, and, as shoes for your feet, having put on the readiness given by the gospel of peace. In all circumstances take up the shield of faith, with which you can extinguish all the flaming darts of the evil one; and take the helmet of salvation, and the sword of the Spirit, which is the word of God, praying at all times in the Spirit, with all prayer and supplication. To that end keep alert with all perseverance, making supplication for all the saints, and also for me, that words may be given to me in opening my mouth boldly to proclaim the mystery of the gospel, for which I am an ambassador in chains, that I may declare it boldly, as I ought to speak".

Let it be clear that God's grace is offered freely to all. That if we have faith in a risen Christ then grace is granted freely to us all and we have received the salvation that Christ's crucifixion earned us. Our savior Jesus Christ still experiences sorrow as he watches upon us because, despite the grace he gives freely to all men, we choose to live a life of the flesh. We refuse to give up our sinful nature and live a life of obedience that is possible by his grace, rather we choose death over life. We refuse to accept the salvation he has earned us freely at no charge save his life. Christ's will is to do the work of his father, and each time we give in to the flesh we are separating ourselves from Christ and disobedient to the will of his father.

Our lord instructs us on his will for all his faithful followers in John 6;39 "And it is the will of him who sent me that I should not lose any of all those he has given me, but that I should raise them all to life on the last day. For what my Father wants is that all who see the Son and believe in him should have eternal life. And I will raise them up on the last day".

Christ's ultimate wish is that every one of his faithful inherit eternal life, each of us matter, our inheritance is that all of the faithful are princes and princesses in our heavenly kingdom now at the end of time. The great gift of faith we have in our one risen Lord, is all that is required for us to be transformed to children of God.

We have established that our bodies are the temple of Christ and that we are one in the Spirit with our Christian brothers and sisters. It is this union with Christ and the church that helps us understand why sins against the flesh have far reaching consequences beyond ourselves alone. By indulging the flesh we reject the salvation that is earned us by Christ's sacrifice at the crucifixion. Our salvation means that sin of any form can no longer separate us from eternal life because we now have the grace that makes us children of God. Christ himself is the sacrifice that saved us from sin and death and earned us eternal life, the faith that we have is what earns us the grace to be called children of God this is why sin has no power over us. Our faith means that we are of the Spirit and not of the flesh ever willing to be obedient to our heavenly Father and welcome his Holy Spirit to dwell within us.

Our faith in a crucified, resurrected Lord who ascended to sit at God's right hand gives us the grace, so that we can die to self, give up our flesh and welcome the Holy Spirit to dwell within us. As Christian brethren we all profess a faith in the one true God; Father, Son and Holy Ghost, however we refuse the grace that is ours freely when we fail to deny the flesh and its earthly needs and welcome the Spirit of our Lord to dwell within us. If we call ourselves Christian yet participate in adultery and fornication, indulge in pornography, are involved in homosexual relationships or commit suicide or abortion then we have turned our back on Christ and refuse to die to our flesh and its needs. As mere mortals we are unable to give up the needs of the flesh, but as soon as we surrender to our Lord and experience the re-birth of our spirit we have been transformed to become true sons of God and can live a life of total submission in true faith.

We can begin to define faith from the word of God in Hebrews 11; 1 Now faith is the assurance of things hoped for, the conviction of things not seen.

If we have no hope of eternal life and have no belief in the death and resurrection of Christ because we are only convinced by what we can see, then we can have no faith. We must never forget that the greatest gift our faith brings us is the grace to be transformed in the spirit to children of God, for only then can we inherit our Father's kingdom.

It is this transformation to children of Spirit that provides us the armor for battle, the regeneration of spirit, renewal of self, the empowerment and innate ability to be children of God. Christ has made all the necessary reparation for our sins, by his life and crucifixion on the cross, ours is to claim the bounty he earned us as we allow him transform us by his grace to faithful children of God.

Mary Magdalene was a woman who lived in sin, but after she encountered Christ she surrendered to him and allowed the Spirit of Christ to transform her and by so doing was re-born to a new life in the Spirit. Christ himself appeared to her after his resurrection and this only confirms that if we give up the sinful nature of our flesh, we will truly be transformed by the Spirit so that we may see the face of Christ and dwell with him in all eternity, this should be our purpose as children of God.

Mark 16;9 Now when he rose early on the first day of the week, he appeared first to Mary Magdalene, from whom he had cast out seven demons.

CHAPTER SEVENTEEN

Sins of the Heart; A bad attitude

Matthew 15; 17-20 "Do you not see that whatever goes into the mouth passes into the stomach and is expelled? But what comes out of the mouth proceeds from the heart, and this defiles a person. For out of the heart come evil thoughts, murder, adultery, sexual immorality, theft, false witness, slander. These are what defile a person. But to eat with unwashed hands does not defile anyone."

It is in our thoughts that we devise our emotions and by our will that we carry out our actions. There is not much we can do to control the thoughts and actions of others but it is by our character that we bear witness to the thoughts and emotion in our hearts. A life in the spirit means that we strive to transform all negative thoughts into thoughts that are uplifting to us as children of the spirit.

At each point in our lives when we are faced with a conflict, we ourselves must determine our reaction to every situation. Our character is often built over the years as we mature from infancy to adulthood. There is no doubt that our genetics and life experiences combine to determine the background on which our character is built. As Christians who are re-born in the Spirit, our new life in the spirit should also reflect in a transformation of our character. Even after we experience this transformation, conflict will continue to come our way as we live through life's experiences. At every opportunity we must each examine our conscience thoroughly and recognize the character traits we possess that are not of the Spirit. As soon as we identify the shortcomings that are ours we must strive to give up the temptation to fall into our old ways and call upon the spirit to strengthen us as we endeavor to walk in the way of the Holy Spirit.

• Envy may rear its head as a feeling of discontent or covetousness with regard to another's possessions, success, personality, wealth or advantages of any form that we desire. Envy goes hand in hand with jealousy and greed, which leads to some form of resentment for whatever advantage or material possession others owns and that we wish to possess ourselves.

Our Lord himself gave us the ninth commandment "You shall not covet your neighbor's house, you shall not covet your neighbor's wife, or his male servant, or his female servant, or his ox, or his donkey, or anything that is your neighbor's." Exodus 20;17

The ninth commandment can be summed up in these few words, 'thou shalt not envy'. Envy in itself is an emotion or feeling but can lead us to lie, steal, cheat or hate which are actions that are not in keeping with a life in the spirit. In as much as envy leads us to examine our conscience and determine in what way we might need to change our attitude or actions so as to work towards achieving goals that are uplifting to us as and to others we might have converted a feeling of envy to one of motivation.

• Greed is the selfish an excessive desire for more of something than is needed. Envy can lead to greed because when we recognize a material possession or attribute another individual owns that we wish to possess it we can begin to have a compulsive desire to obtain it at all costs, regardless of what sin we are led to commit in order to attain it. Greed is the thermostat that indicates we are not satisfied with what we have even when it is enough. If we chose to transform greed into an inspiration to strive to improve ourselves in whatever way is necessary so as to acquire our needs rather than become so consumed with hate or anger we are living in the spirit of God.

• Jealousy is a strong feeling of possessiveness, often caused by the possibility that something which belongs, or ought to belong to one is about to be taken away. Jealousy is not in keeping with a life in the spirit when it leads us to hate our brothers and sisters.

After Cain and Able had made an offering to the Lord, Cain was filled with jealousy and envy towards his brother because his offering was found unworthy by the Lord while his brother's was found worthy. Cain could have let his jealousy and envy motivate him to do better and make a worthy offering to the Lord, but rather, Cane chose to kill his brother after he chose to let his jealousy and envy lead him to hate and anger.

Genesis 4;6-8 The Lord said to Cain, "Why are you angry, and why has your face fallen? If you do well, will you not be accepted? And if you do not do well, sin is crouching at the door. Its desire is for you, but you must rule over it". Cain spoke to Abel his brother. And when they were in the field, Cain rose up against his brother Abel and killed him.

Jacob stole from his father the blessing of the first born son which should have been for his twin brother Esau, and he was aided in this deception by his mother Rebekah. This caused Esau to be angry and hate his brother, understandably so, but as children of the spirit we cannot allow anger lead us to hate and must learn to call upon the spirit as we seek for strength and wisdom when faced with adversity. Jacob did well to remove himself from his brother's presence after offending him, as he fled to his uncle Laban after he heard Esau planned to kill him, it is appropriate after a sufficient cool off time to try and resolve such a conflict like Esau and Jacob did eventually.

Genesis 27; 41-45 Now Esau hated Jacob because of the blessing with which his father had blessed him, and Esau said to himself, "The days of mourning for my father are approaching; then I will kill my brother Jacob." When Rebekah was told what her older son Esau had said, she sent for hey younger son Jacob and said to him, "Your brother Esau is planning to avenge himself by killing you. Now then, my son, do what I say; Flee at once to my brother Laban in Harran. Stay with him a while until your brother's fury subsides. When your brother is no longer angry with you and forgets what you did to him, I'll send word for you to come back from there. Why should I lose both of you in one day?"

The story of 'Cain and Abel' and 'Esau and Jacob' illustrates how jealousy, envy and greed can lead to a hate that is destructive and cause us to sin. Jealousy and envy can cause us to hate another individual due to the perceived threat we feel we face and also when we become so possessive about material possessions that we have no desire to share it or are prepared to lie, steal, kill or cheat in an attempt to poses that which belongs to another. When jealousy greed and envy lead us to examine our conscience and we transform it to the positive emotion of sharing or when it causes us to act in a way that is just and upright to achieve a goal that is uplifting to us as an individual then we have transformed it to a character in keeping with a life in the spirit.

• Cynicism is an attitude of scornful or jaded negativity that causes us to question a positive outcome and always expect the worst. Our faith as Christian's causes us to see a positive outcome in all situations even if it is one we can only hope for it. Our belief is that as children of God he watches over us and protects us always and this means that we only experience trials if our Lord allows it and only if it will work together with our Lord's plan for our salvation. If we are cynical then we question the Spirit of Christ that is at play in all situations that arise in our lives and we cannot have the hope that all things will work together for our good because of the faith and love we have for our savior Jesus Christ. Cynicism is the direct opposite of faith and is not in keeping with a life in the spirit.

As previously stated faith is defined in the book of Hebrews 11;1 Now faith is the assurance of things hoped for, the conviction of things not seen.

• Selfishness is synonymous with self-centeredness and is manifested by caring only for oneself, concern primarily with own interests and a disregard for the needs of others. Selfishness goes against our creed as children of God who should be known for the love we have for our Lord and the love we have for one another.

1 John 3;17 But if anyone has the world's good and sees his brother in need, yet closes his heart against him, how does God's love abide in him.

Our Lord Jesus Christ showed us the true meaning of the world love when he gave up his life for us on the cross that we may have salvation he was absolutely selfless. As children of God we also should be willing to put the needs of others before ourselves in as long as we do no unbearable harm to ourselves when we do that. If we only desire to satisfy our needs regardless of the consequences to others then we are being self-centered and this is not in keeping with a life in the spirit. Selfishness goes against the generosity of heart and material possessions we should have as Christians. Loving our neighbor means we reach out and help when we see anyone in need, even if we have to go out of our way and cause a little inconvenience to ourselves. If we only seek for our own comforts and have no desire to share this with others or help them to achieve their own comforts then we are selfish and in need of the transformation of Spirit that all children of God need to experience so that we can truly live in the spirit as children of God. As a child of God you have to be prepared to understand that it is not all bout you all the time, if the Lord has enabled us then we should use our gifts to enable others for this is how we show love. A true love for our Lord and our neighbor is synonymous with self-sacrifice and generosity.

2Timothy 3; 1-5 But understand this, that in the last days there will comes times of difficulty. For people will be lovers of self, lovers of money, proud, arrogant, abusive, disobedient to their parents, ungrateful, unholy, heartless, unappeasable, slanderous, without self-control, brutal, not loving good, treacherous, reckless, swollen with conceit, lovers of pleasure rather than lovers of God, having the appearance of godliness, but denying its power. Avoid such people.

• Evil suspicion or paranoia may stem from life experiences that have caused us to distrust or expect the worst from others. In situations where we have been disappointed it is appropriate to be prepared for the worst in our expectations from certain individuals but we cannot go through life always suspicious and expecting the worst even where we have no cause to. We learn as we mature as Christians to trust in the Lord alone, we also come to realize that our Lord works through individuals who allow him to use them as servants of his work. As long as individuals we are called upon to trust are spirit filled and servants of the Lord we can learn to trust them as doers of God's work even as we pray that the Lord will strengthen them to uphold the faith they profess. To be suspicious and paranoid means we are extremely fearful of harm and expect the worst at all times. No child of God should live in fear, we should pray instead for the spirit of discernment that the Lord will open our eyes to recognize those who are not true to their faith by their actions.

1 Timothy 6; 3-5 If anyone teaches a different doctrine and does not agree with the sound words of our Lord Jesus Christ and the teaching that accords with godliness, he is puffed up with conceit and understands nothing. He has an unhealthy craving

for controversy and for quarrels about words, which produce envy, dissension, slander, evil suspicions, and constant friction amongst people who are depraved in mind and deprived of the truth, imagining that godliness is a means of gain.

We all know that Christ sat at the table and ate with Judas Iscariot before he was betrayed by him, there is no doubt that the Lord knew who was to betray him when they sat to eat at the last supper for he recognized that the one to betray him was sitting with him at the table. But Christ did not let this discernment lead him to hate or anger, we also must learn to use this gift of the spirit to caution and correct one another, or at the very least pray for each other. Christ himself cautioned Judas, but his greed caused a hardened heart that did not allow him to repent of his evil plan.

Luke 22; 21-23" But behold, the hand of him who betrays me is with me on the table. For the son of man goes as it has been determined, but woe to that man by whom he is betrayed!" And they began to question another, which of them it could be who was going to do this.

There is no doubt in my mind that Judas had stolen from the purse of the Apostles severally as the purse keeper. As with all sins against the body once we begin to fall to sin that our ego tells us are small and do no harm, there is no doubt that we silence our conscience and lose the voice of the Holy Spirit within. Perhaps this is why Judas could fall into the temptation of greed and betray Christ for thirty silver pieces. If we feel our brothers or sisters act in a manner that causes us to question their loyalty then we should caution them and remind them of the scripture that should guide our actions as children of God. If they fail to take correction then we must inform elders in the church or family who can further examine our actions and judge fairly, they can then intervene if necessary so as to keep the peace that should exist between brethren. In a situation where an individual is offended but feels able to let it go and bear no malice then it is appropriate to forgive the offender even while we commit ourselves to the Lord in prayer. We must not let suspicion and paranoia stand in the way of our salvation.

James 1;19 Know this, my beloved brothers; let every person be quick to hear, slow to speak, slow to anger.

• Anger can lead us to zeal and this may be keeping with our Lord's purpose when it causes us to act in accordance with the word of God.

John 2; 14-17 In the temple he found those who were selling oxen and sheep and pigeons, and the money-changers sitting there. And making a whip of cords, he drove them all out of the temple, with the sheep and oxen. And he poured out the coins of the money-changers and overturned their tables. And he told those who sold the pigeons, "Take these things away; do not make my Father's house a house of trade." His disciples remembered that it was written, "Zeal for your house will consume me."

When anger leads us to hate or causes us to hurt others be it physically or emotionally then this is not in keeping with a life in the spirit. We must remember that as children of the spirit we should exercise self-control at all times. The self-control that we have does not mean that we deny our feelings, it just means that we express them in a manner that is respectful even when we get passionate or upset about issues. Self-control means that we guard our thoughts, hearts and tongue and that we do not allow our anger lead to hate, malice, gossip, disobedience or hurt in any form.

Ephesians 4;31-32 Let all bitterness and wrath and anger and clamor and slander be put away from you, along with all malice. Be kind to one another, tenderhearted, forgiving one another, as God in Christ forgave you.

We must always attempt to express our grievances and try to resolve them amicably, where this is not possible we may inform spirit filled family members or friends to intervene with their wisdom as we continue to attempt to resolve conflict. In situations where an issue cannot be resolved in a manner that is amicable it may be appropriate to take a time out as we continue to take it to our Lord in prayer, we may then attempt to resolve these issues in the future after our passions and emotions have been brought under self-control.

1 Corinthians 13;4 Love is patient and kind; love does not envy or boast; it is not arrogant.

- Pride is the exact opposite of humility, when we fail to recognize that all that we have that is good comes from God, we are prideful. Even when we feel we have worked hard and achieved our goal we must continue to remember that it is the Lord that blesses the work of our hands. We may plant the seed and water the fields, but it is only by our Lord's grace that we reap a good harvest. We must not forget to give our Lord the glory for the great harvests he gives us in our life. It is only if we are humble and recognize Christ as the source of our success that we can give him back the glory he so deserves. And it is only if we are humble that we can recognize our limitations as children of the flesh and die to our flesh and its needs so that we may rise to a new life in the spirit. Pride that has an origin in our own abilities is not in keeping with a life in spirit. Our pride as children of God should be one that is humble, every thankful and grateful to our Lord.

1 John 2;16 For all that is in the world – the desires of the flesh and the desires of the eyes and pride of life - is not from the father but is from the world.

There is no doubt that the emotions of envy, greed, jealousy, cynicism, selfishness, self-centeredness, evil suspicion, paranoia, anger and pride can cause conflict in our lives as Christian's. We must strive to resolve these conflicts where ever possible and by the grace of the spirit transform them into a character that is in keeping with a life in the spirit such as kindness, compassion, contentment, generosity, motivation, loyalty, trust, self-control and humility. As long as our daily needs are met we must learn to guard our thoughts so that we do not begin to obsess about possessions that are not necessary to us. Our new life in the spirit must shine forth in our love for our neighbor, good attitude, behavior and character at all times and in all situations.

Colossians 3; 8-10,12-14 But now you must put them all way; anger, wrath, malice, slander and obscene talk from your mouth. Do not lie to one another, seeing that you have put off the old self with all its practices and have put on the new self, which is being renewed in knowledge after the image of the creator. Put on then, as God's chosen ones, holy and beloved, compassionate hearts, kindness, humility, meekness, and patience, bearing with one another and, if one has a complaint against another, forgiving each other; as the Lord has forgiven you, so you also must forgive. And above all these things put on love which binds everything together in perfect harmony.

CHAPTER EIGHTEEN

Suicide

The Lord gives us a commandment; Exodus 20;13 You shall not commit murder.

We must understand that God gives life; he alone is the creator, author and finisher of life. To take the life of any human being including self is an action of great disobedience to our father. True obedience means that we obey not only the word that appeals to us, but all of God's word. What makes us Christian is the love we have for self, love for God, love for our brothers and sisters, love for all of God's creation. Any act that leads a person to destroy himself and take his own life is against our faith as Christians.

Suicide is the intentional taking of one's own life. After haven clarified that the body is the temple of the Lord and understanding that as true Christians we must surrender ourselves to the Lord's will. We can have no doubt that suicide is a sin against our body, the body of Christ and his entire Church. Suicide leads to a death of the physical form but releases the spirit form to receive the final judgment. If we understand that the final judgment may lead us to an unquenchable fire we must take the opportunity of life to reconcile ourselves with our Lord who is ever waiting to receive us back into his fold. Suicide is not the way to end the anguish we experience within, the mere thought of suicide is an indication that it is time to seek help from our Priests and pastors as well as qualified mental health professionals.

Suicide bombing is a sin against the body but often also results in murder usually of innocent bystanders. Suicide bombers often have a cause which they support which is often times religious. They partake in the act of suicide bombing as a method of instilling terror on others as well as to achieve desired goals for their cause. Suicide bombers have a misguided notion that sacrificing their lives is a form of martyrdom and they will end up in eternal paradise. These individuals are often indoctrinated with extremist propaganda to the extent where they no longer have any consideration for the innocent lives they sacrifice as well as their own; they develop sociopathic personalities, a total lack of compassion or thoughtfulness for others, a disregard for God's law and the law of the land. There is no doubt that a suicide bomber has silenced their conscience and allowed their flesh to be used as an instrument of evil.

Self-euthanasia is a form of suicide where one intentionally takes one's own life to end suffering and pain from terminal illness. It is important that we surround ourselves with persons we love when faced with terminal illness. True love means that we can trust our close family, friends and church members to care for us and carry out our living will as directed. Our ultimate trust is in our heavenly Lord though he provides care for us through our loved ones. A terminal illness is a true test of faith but when we undergo this trial by fire we must not lose sight of our faith which means that as we carry our cross we know that our Lord will continue to watch over us until our last breath. It is our Lord who gives us life and we must return to him in true repentance, humility, faith and trust when the end of life on earth draws near.

Suicide regardless of the cause is undoubtedly an outward act arising from an inner anguish. It is a last act of one who feels life is not worth living. Various circumstances and personalities that are border line given to extremes of emotion may cause a person to feel a sense of guilt and inner turmoil that may be delusional as it often appears to exceed the gravity of the offence committed. Just as the sense of shame can lead to repentance, despair, justification or denial, the sense of guilt can do the same. Unfortunately in situations where a sense of guilt leads to despair, an individual might come to feel worthless, unworthy of forgiveness and feel that life is no longer worth living. The danger of an individual considering a perceived offence so grievous as to be unforgivable is that such an individual is unable to begin the process of repentance since one cannot get past the offence committed. An individual who feels he is not worthy of forgiveness by God might also feel he is not worthy of forgiveness by others. One cannot begin the process of repentance and forgiveness of sin if one cannot forgive oneself. The insight of persons committing suicide is often impaired because they perceive that there is no solution to the inner anguish they experience, hence they fail to seek help.

An individual experiencing the emotion of extreme anger, rage, guilt or depression might experience such an intense sense of despair that they feel life is no longer worth living. At any point where thoughts of suicide occur it is necessary to share these thoughts with a pastor, priest, family member or mental health professional that is capable of providing the required counselling at this time. If these thoughts are not addressed and an individual goes a step further to begin to formulate or carry out a plan on a method of suicide then it is necessary at this point that such an individual be removed from the stressful environment and be supervised by the appropriate mental health personnel as there is an increased likelihood of carrying out a plan. An individual committing suicide as a form of 'acting out' might have the intention of causing anguish to whosoever committed a perceived wrongdoing or as a means to put an end to the anguish, despair or depression that one feels. These individuals might also have poor insight and bad judgment and hence may not be capable of processing the fact that suicide is permanent and irreversible. Any thoughts or plans of suicide must not be taken lightly and is a sure indication that an individual is in need of professional help.

The prodigal son had to consider in his thoughts that his father would accept him albeit as a lowly servant, he had a fleeting return of his insight that spurred him to return to his father and ask for forgiveness. In the same way as children of God, we must understand that Christ is not only wiling, but ever ready and pleased to forgive us, regardless of whatever sin we may have committed. The negative voice within us that tell us we are not worthy of forgiveness is definitely a spirit that is not of the Lord. Christ died for us on the cross forgiving us even as he bled for us on the cross and we crucified him. Our Lord is a forgiving God; he loves us even more so when we are sinners, for if we are without sin we would have no need for salvation. We often feel Christ can only love us if we are perfect and without sin, but then his death would have been in vain. Christ died for us precisely for this reason; because we are sinners. For if the Lord were to judge us by the law, no one would receive salvation because as man we sin again and again and have fallen short of his glory. Certain individuals might have fallen so deep into despair, self-blame, and guilt that they are unable to ask for help, it is imperative that family members or friends who recognize this lead such individuals to the appropriate mental and spiritual help that they need.

Galatians 2;16, 21; "Yet we know that a person is put right with God only through faith in Jesus Christ, never by doing what the law requires. I refuse to reject the grace of God. But if a person is put right with God through the law, it means that Christ died for nothing".

Gal3:5 "Does God give you the spirit and work miracles among you because you do what the Lord requires or because you hear the gospel and believe it"

If it is Christ's crucifixion that has earned us salvation, then we all have been given the birth-rite to be called sons of God; as children of God, we should be confident that our Father would never leave us without help. A feeling of guilt that leads unto death instead of salvation can only exist when we question God's love for us, or when we feel that salvation is earned us by keeping the law and living without sin. We must never question the love that our Lord has for us. There is repeated evidence of God's love for man, and his willingness to forgive us repeatedly in scripture. If we are convinced that Christ loves us even more, when we are sinners, then we must never allow guilt or shame lead us to suicide. If we know that we earn salvation by our faith and not by keeping the law, there is no other proof we need that our Lord is ever willing to forgive us. If we acknowledge that our Lord is always willing to forgive us and wishes us to inherit eternal life then all we have to do is acknowledge our sin and ask for forgiveness with a true and contrite heart. Suicide is never an option for a true living son of God, we must share the word of God and pray without seizing in times of despair that the Holy Spirit may touch our hearts and cause us to regain an insight of the love the Lord has for us and that it is unconditional.

Any individual contemplating suicide must not hesitate to seek help from qualified health care professionals, Priests, Pastors and counsellors in the church who are filled with the wisdom of the Holy Spirit. At times of despair let us not cease to remember that it is at times like this that we are the wandering sheep that Christ repeatedly referred to and that even as we suffer he is leaving the ninety-nine sheep in his fold to seek for us the one roaming sheep.

We must always endeavor to retain the self-esteem and confidence that is our birth-rite as children of God which arises from the fact that even when we were sinners Christ died for us to show how much he loved us and even as we wander he seeks and awaits our return. Suicide is not in keeping with a life in the spirit of our Lord and anyone considering such an option should immediately seek for help and call a friend.

CHAPTER NINETEEN

Pedophilia

Matthew 18: 6 - If anyone should cause one of these little ones to lose his faith in me, it would be better for that person to have a large millstone tied around his neck and be drowned in the deep sea. How terrible for the world that there are things that make people lose their faith! Such things will always happen – but how terrible for the one who causes them!

Child abuse of any kind is not in keeping with life in the Spirit of God. Child sexual abuse is the sexual mistreatment of a child and there is no doubt that this is an act that cannot in any way be rationalized. Child sexual abuse is the evidence of the worst evil we are capable of as humans. I believe this is the lowest we can go, the farthest we can fall, the worst that man can be is to carry out the act of child abuse of any form on any child.

Offenders of child sexual abuse are referred to as pedophiles, child rapists or, child molesters. In cases where child sexual abuse is committed against a child that is related to the perpetrator, this is referred to as incest. Regardless of the term by which they are labeled, these offenders are sexual predators to children. What can make man perform such a dastardly act that is so irrational?

This evil undoubtedly derives from the mind. The fact that a child is defenseless, cannot protect themselves physically and also may be easily influenced by persons in authority, makes this all the more intolerable. That anyone would defile a child the epitome of the innocence of man, the most Christ like of all humans surely means that any child predator has silenced his conscience, which is the spirit of God or the voice of God within them.

Individuals without a sense of judgment, who have an inability to define right from wrong, are often termed sociopaths. I however, refuse to refer to child abuse perpetrators as sociopaths, simply because they are aware that what they do is wrong. Child abusers do not perform these lewd acts publicly and will only carry out these acts after detailed planning and usually have preexisting intent. A sociopath on the other hand has no regard for the law and often lives a life that is dysfunctional and is easily recognized as an unsavory character. Unlike sociopaths, child abuse perpetrators are often respected members of the community, sane enough to be functional, carry out everyday tasks, are often welcomed into our homes and are able to bring children into their confidence simply for the fact that they appear to care for children. Unfortunately these predators are trusted members of society, hence they are often granted free access to children on the premise of being authority figures such as Priests, coaches on teams, parents or care providers that are responsible for the children under their care.

The question then becomes, how can a person of sound mind, commit such a crime as this? Let us first of all clarify that as previously established, the mind of a child abuser is no longer sound because the conscience which is the spirit voice within them is silenced hence they have lost all sense of insight and are deaf to the words of the spirit. Child molesters rationalize their bad behavior and live in denial. Child predators are alive in the flesh but dead in the spirit as they refuse to listen to the voice of the Spirit.

This impaired sense of judgment and insight is albeit solely in the area of child molestation, as child predators often appear to have an intact sense of judgment in other aspects of their life. Child predators recognize their desires as unacceptable because their conscience tells them this but they eventually silence their conscience by repeatedly ignoring it and justifying their impulses. Child molesters may feel a certain shame for harboring thoughts in their mind of sexually abusing children however, rather than allow this shame to bring them to confession of sin and repentance, they overcome their shame by denial. Denial comes from a spirit of the flesh and is not of God and is quite a tame word for a state of mind that has such dire consequences and brings such pain to innocent children. Ignoring the voice of God within us is the sure way to cause death to our conscience or insight. As a predator contemplates such evil acts as child abuse, such a person can decide by their own free will to be obedient to God's word or to dwell on these evil thoughts and subsequently begin to fantasize about these thoughts. Once a predator allows these thoughts to dwell in the mind willingly, the sequence of child sexual molestation has been set in motion. Predators of child abuse, who should abstain from communication and isolation with a child knowing very well the temptations that they experience and the thoughts in their minds, instead begin to find a way to bring children into their confidence. They may buy children gifts, as a way to win the affection or respect of a child. Child predators will seek opportunities to have children isolated and alone in their presence, they might volunteer to provide free child care, just for the opportunity to be isolated with a child. They often seek out occupations that put them in direct contact with children such as bus drivers, coaches on a team, teachers and child minders. They may appear more "cool" or tolerant to a child, whose own parents due to establishing discipline may appear unsympathetic or hard to a child. These predators may seem to look out for a child or be concerned about a child's welfare. Predators however, once they have won a child into their confidence look for an opportunity to be isolated with a child and take that opportunity to perform acts of child sexual abuse against that child. Predators might also abduct a child so as to have absolute power over a child and repeatedly abuse them. These thoughts of child sexual abuse often can begin in the thoughts during the age of adolescence and predators may have begun experimenting with child sexual abuse from the age of adolescence up till adulthood. If predators seeks to indulge these thoughts their behavior may escalate as they further explore their fantasies and a mere observing or 'looking' at kids, may soon escalate to inappropriate exposure, then touching and eventually rape.

The recent trend of child sexual abuse by Priests in the Catholic Church leads one to ask, 'How can Priests, disciples of Christ, doers of God's work, justify such an unholy act as this. If any being should have a sense of what is right or wrong in God's sight, it should be none other than a Priest. Priests are representatives of Christ on earth, as disciples of Christ they are well informed and versed in God's word. How does a Priest silence the conscience within him, lose all sense of judgment and insight, live in denial and begin to justify the evil of child sexual abuse? Nothing, absolutely nothing can justify this unholy act. There is no doubt that many Priests might have been raised in an environment of child sexual abuse and were sexually abused as children, sometimes by older Priests. Abuse as a child can predispose one to be without a conscience against child sexual abuse simply due to the environment in which they were raised. If there is no clear separation of wrong from right in childhood, then an individual might truly have been raised with the conscience, which is the spirit within him, silenced. Hence, this vicious cycle often repeats itself. Children who have been sexually abused can often become abusers of children if they do not receive the counseling and help they need.

Priests might also have been secluded for prolonged periods in seminaries where they receive theological education and Priestly training. During this time of seclusion as adolescents, or young adults, they might have engaged in self-exploration and sexual exploration of other individuals, creating a breeding ground for submission to flesh rather than submission to the Holy Spirit. If shame causes a Priest to confess and repent of this behavior they grow up to be healthy well-adjusted adult priests, however if they live in denial and begin to justify their behavior, they soon lose all sense of judgment and justify this behavior, and repeatedly perform such acts. Once, secluded as Priests in Parishes, they are in positions of authority and have children under their care. Priests may soon abuse this position by taking advantage of children, once they have the opportunity of isolation with a child. There is no doubt that children who are emotionally fragile, neglected children, orphans, abandoned children might be targets of Priest perpetrators as they view such children as less likely to expose their un-priestly behavior and easier to convince that such acts are acceptable by virtue of their emotional fragility.

Priests as ambassadors of Christ on earth are also no doubt target of the devil and his angels prowling the world seeking the destruction of souls. If the devil allows such impure thoughts to fester in the mind of Priests, then they of all beings should know that if they welcome such thoughts and allow thoughts of child sexual abuse to dwell in their minds, they are disobedient to God's word and have lost all sense of judgment. Consent to isolation then sets the stage for sexual abuse of a child or minor in their charge. Priests who fail to bring their impulses sunder control continue to commit this dastardly act.

There is no excuse that can excuse this dastardly action by any persons or Priest, any adult who faces this temptation of child sexual abuse must seek immediate help and desist from any form of contact with children

In certain instances, due to a life of self-indulgence, sexually deviant behavior such as sexual orgies, indulging in child pornography or pornography of any kind we have succeeded in silencing the Holy Spirit within us. We then lose all sense of judgment, deny our inappropriate behavior, and begin to justify our indecent human desires, that are against the spirit of Christ. At this point we have by our own will, chosen to indulge in sinful desires rather than obedience to God's word. We lose all sense of guilt or shame by justifying our behavior, lying to our own selves.

A child predator lives a life that is one of denial, because on the surface they appear to have a life of normalcy, might be great volunteers and people of importance or at least significance in the community, however, in their spirit they are dead to life and without a conscience. Child predators have perfected the act of denial to the extent that they attempt to rationalize their sinful behavior by convincing themselves that they are causing no harm to the child, tell themselves that they are showing love to the child. Feel that the child involved is gaining some benefit from this experience, that they have no choice because thy experienced this as children themselves. One common thought by which child predators rationalize their behavior, is by suggesting that it is not them but the devil that is responsible for the evil they have done, the devil can only take possession of our souls if we refuse to listen to our conscience, by refusing to listen to our conscience which is the voice of God within us, we have inadvertently chosen to listen to the devil. We alone control our will, so we alone have to take responsibility for our actions. It is important to understand how child abuse predators rationalize their behavior because this is how they convince themselves that what they do is right and hence repeatedly commit this vile act.

Apart from losing all sense of judgment and insight as regards the act of child abuse, pedophiles also become experts at self-detachment, almost like they adopt multiple personalities, the evil child molester by night, and the upright citizen at daytime. As with all sins against the body once we have given up the struggle, refused to allow shame lead us to obedience and silence the needs of the flesh we have sold our soul to the devil. Child molesters rationalize their behavior then develop a certain detachment and are so lacking in a conscience that they can take up the semblance of a normal life while secretly performing such atrocious acts. The moment an individual performs the act of child abuse to a child there is no doubt that he has given up the battle, evil has conquered good, darkness has conquered light, by his own will, he allows the act of child sexual abuse to occur due to the denial by which he rationalizes his behavior.

There should be no doubt that immediately thoughts of child abuse of any form enter the mind one must immediately reject such a thought or feeling as unnatural and proclaim it as such then through prayer and the word of God submit to the Holy Spirit and let him lead you to overcome such thoughts. It becomes paramount that we seek help once we find that these thoughts repeatedly come into our minds and we cannot suppress such thoughts from our minds. Christ himself said to Peter his Apostle: "Be gone from me Satan"- Matthew 4:10, when Peter suggested that Christ reconsider drinking of the cup which was his crucifixion. It is in this same vain that we must reject any thoughts suggesting such lewd acts. If we allow such thoughts to fester in our hearts or mind, and do not reject them out rightly, then we are indirectly welcoming evil into our hearts. As adults we have to understand that we must be accountable for our actions. Each time we welcome such unholy feelings as arousal to childhood indiscreet photos we are further silencing the spirit within us in our conscience, and as always follows silencing the conscience, we begin to rationalize our bad behavior. Encouraging such thoughts and repeating such behavior soon results in addiction to such behavior or action making the body becomes a slave to its own desires.

All sins against the body are sins against the body of Christ which is his church and sin against Christ in his flesh. The consequences of this sin against a child are far beyond that of any other kind of sin against the body. Christ is indeed merciful and always ready to forgive us if our contrition is true and real. If one tries to repeal such evil spirit thoughts and has no success, then it becomes necessary to call for help from spiritual directors in the church, Pastors or Priests and mental health personnel to pray with one and support one in bringing such evil thoughts under control. Often prayer and fasting are needed and the support of the body of Christ, and Christ himself as flesh and as Spirit. As with all sins against the body it is also important to recognize that child sexual abuse does not occur in public. No individual experiencing such thoughts should allow himself be isolated with a child, until such thoughts or feelings are brought under the dominion of the Holy Spirit.

Mark 9: 25 - After healing a deaf and dumb child, Christ's disciples asked him, why couldn't we drive the spirit out? 'Only prayer can drive this kind out, answered Jesus, 'nothing else can'.

Have we called upon spiritual directors in church, our Pastor or Priest, have they prayed with us, laid hands upon us, fasted with us and yet we are unable to overcome such thoughts, then what next, Christ himself gives us the answer in this verse.

Matthew 18: 8 - If your hand or your foot makes you lose your faith, cut it off and throw it away! It is better for you to enter life without a hand or a foot than to keep both hands and both feet and be thrown into eternal fire. And if your eyes make you lose your faith, take it out and throw it away! It is better for you to enter life with only one eye than to keep both eyes and be thrown into the fire of hell.

No doubt we physically put ourselves in a place often in isolation where such lewd acts are performed, one needs to check oneself while in public, do not allow yourself to be led by evil to commit evil acts. The act of putting oneself in the presence of a child, making contact with a child, these are the point where we have a chance to make the right decision, better to pluck the eye out than use it to lust in an inappropriate manner. With child pornography or giving a child lewd looks, this is another opportunity to check ourselves and protect our eyes and senses, we must guard our sight and only look at images that can uplift us physically and spiritually not send us to sensual thoughts that are absolutely inappropriate. Extremely inappropriate actions sometimes need to be brought under control by extreme measures, this is definitely called for in the situation of temptations to commit the act of child sexual abuse. Though Christ was literal in his statement when he said 'if your eye causes you to sin, pluck it out. If your hand or foot causes you to sin, cut it off'. Persons who have found that they cannot bring inappropriate sensual impulses under control and lust after children as well as seeking spiritual support also should be aware that medical treatment by health personnel is necessary and available ranging from psychotherapy to medications which help us bring our impulses under control. The physical act of castration may no longer be practiced as a form of controlling inappropriate sexual attraction to children, however, chemical castration with medication that suppress testosterone levels are quite effective in controlling sexual drive in men. True, these measures may seem extreme, but extreme situations are often brought under control by extreme measures.

There is no doubt that the choice is ours to make, does one continue to live in denial and justify lewd acts such as child sexual abuse, or will such a person recognize the error of his ways, make reparation, turn himself or herself in to the authorities and ask forgiveness from the Lord.

The Lord awaits us with open arms to welcome all back into his fold, he is not Lord only of the righteous, but Lord also of sinners. The Father did not send the son to bring back to him the sheep that were wandering the pasture at home, no, he sent the good shepherd to find the lost sheep. It is for the likes of you and me that he gave his life. May pride, denial and justifying of child abuse tendencies, not stand in the way of the truth that leads to our salvation. Child abuse of any form is not in keeping with life in the spirit of our Lord.

CHAPTER TWENTY

Adultery, Fornication or Prostitution

Thou shall not commit adultery, Exodus 20;14.

• Adultery is the act of sexual intercourse between a married person and someone other than their spouse.

• Fornication refers to consensual sexual intercourse between unmarried persons.

• Prostitution is the business or practice of using our bodies to provide sensual services to another person in return for some form of payment. Pornography, pole dancing, nude dancing, escort services, all put us in an environment that causes us to use our bodies in a sensual way to derive some material gain. If we have come to the conclusion that our bodies as children of God serve as temples of our Lord, we must treat the Lord's abode with due respect, and only use it in a way that is in harmony with God's plan for creation.

In modern times adolescents frequently enter into a relationship once they have a mutual liking for each other, this might be termed 'going out' or 'seeing' each other. This liking may soon give way to desire and hence the act of fornication becomes a temptation. As children of God who seek to do his will all Christian adolescents should abstain from sensual indulgence until marriage. Recognizing the sensual feeling of desire as a precursor to fornication should cause us to caution ourselves before we give in to desire. In any relationship before a desire begins to exist to take things to the next level of intimacy this is the time to set the rules and communicate our intent and desires with our partner and draw up a relationship agreement or contract. It is advisable that all meetings between individuals in a pre-marital relationship occur in a public place or in the presence of a chaperone. The word Chaperone connotes a third party who might be a friend or family member that serves as a buffer during all meetings.

Where there is a desire to do the right thing and the will to succeed, there is definitely a way. Be aware that continuing in a relationship where both individuals are like minded has a higher chance of succeeding than a relationship where only one individual is against fornication. If we proceed in a relationship with a partner who has no interest in abstinence then the risk of failing into the temptation of fornication exists. A true love of God and an understanding that our bodies are holy temples of the Lord is enough reason to abstain.

1Cor 6; 15-17 Do you not know that your bodies are members of Christ? Shall I then take the members of Christ and make them members of a prostitute? Never! Or do you not know that he who is joined to a prostitute becomes one body with her? For as it is written "the two will become one flesh". But he who is joined to the Lord becomes one spirit with him

Once the body is partaking in sins against the body such as fornication or adultery, we lose a sense of self –esteem and pride that we should possess as children of God. We must preserve our virtue at all costs, to keep ourselves as temples holy and worthy of Christ. We must not fail to understand that once the act of fornication has occurred if we continue in such a relationship the risk of repeating this act is quite high. As with all sins against the body once we repeatedly commit this act we lose our sense of judgment and often begin to justify our actions. As children of God we must be bold and upstanding in all our actions.

Adolescence is a time when we are filled with passion and have time on our hands. This is also a time to foster a relationship with the Lord that is unlike the relationship we might have had as children. We make a conscious decision to serve the Lord, to abide in his word as we study his word with a deeper understanding. We can dedicate our time and efforts to doing God's work and spreading his word and performing acts of charity. These formative years are a time to discover ourselves, determine our beliefs and what we stand for until such a time as we may be called to marriage. While in a relationship if we discover attributes in our partner that are unsavory we are in a position to put a halt to the relationship if we deem it fit. A relationship is a time to discover each other's personality and character and to grow in a deeper understanding of each other. Sexual intercourse is actually not a part of a premarital relationship and should only occur after marriage. Adolescence is the time when we are mature enough to begin a relationship with Christ whereby we die to the flesh and no longer desire to fulfill our own needs and wants, but to live according to the Lord's precepts. We must hold on to our virtue until we trust our partner enough and have matured enough to marry each other. We must not live in sin if we desire to serve as God's temple and follow the teachings of Christ.

As a physician I advise abstinence until marriage for all adolescents but offer contraception to adolescents who refuse this option and have chosen to become sexually active, condoms to avoid sexually transmitted diseases and contraception to prevent pregnancy after counseling on the virtues of abstinence. It is by our own will that we have to consent to abstinence, adolescents cannot be forced to remain abstinent, they must desire this of their own free will. A true love for Christ and an understanding of how indulging the flesh can separate us from Christ and expose us to sexually transmitted diseases and pregnancy should deter us from the temptation of fornication or adultery.

By adolescence most individuals have already come to their own conclusion regarding pre-marital sex, this is why the communication should begin during early teenage years so that all teenagers can understand how they are God's temple and should remain holy as temples of God. The reason we must value virtue is because we love our Lord and wish to be willing temples, not because of a fear of pregnancy or sexually transmitted diseases alone. It is the role of all parents and religious leaders to teach children the value of their virtue, long before they become adolescents. Yes, they must understand the risks associated with pre-marital sex and how to protect themselves but my hope is that they will value their virtue enough as a worthy offering to our Lord, and offer themselves as holy temples until such a time as they marry. This might seem impossible, however with the tools our Lord offers freely to all; his grace, baptism by water and the holy spirit, his body and blood, prayer and communication we will find that every adolescent is empowered and able to do what is right in the Lord's sight.

Pre-adolescence is the time to empower ourselves with the tools that are freely given by the Lord so that our faith is manifested in our character and choices.

Shame and fear often cause adolescents to live in denial; they become sexually active, but do not communicate this to their parents, guardians or health care providers. The onus is on all guardians and youth ministry teachers to communicate with pre-adolescents provide them with the right tools so that they are well informed to make the right choice. The grace of the Lord is available to all adolescents who desire to live in the Spirit. We must respect each adolescent as their own person with their own rights and our primary role is to support them in whatever decision they make regarding their personal choices.

If we truly have faith, then we know that Christ will always provide for us, he will not abandon us in our time of need. Turning to prostitution as a means of livelihood is a sure sign that we lack faith in the Lord's ability to provide for us. If an individual feels pushed to the wall and has no other options to provide for self and family, then it might be time to approach elders in the church, our Pastor or Priest, doers of God's work or family members for help. This is why the church exists as one body, to support and provide for each other in our time of need. As females with a sense of self-worth we should always aim to empower ourselves by gaining an education as a means to support ourselves and our families, we often need support while we educate ourselves or try to acquire a skill to support ourselves. As the body of Christ understanding that sin against one body is a sin against the entire body and Christ himself we would be hypocrites if we are not willing to support a female who would rather live an upright life than become a prostitute. The time for change is now, we are required to do what is right in the eye of God and he will surely grant us the grace by his Spirit and provide us support through our likeminded brothers and sisters. This change has to begin with an individual by our own will, deciding to do what is right according to God's word. The church also has to do what is right by providing support to females who are unable to fend for themselves while at the same time educating them with skills and trades that serve as viable ways to earn a livelihood.

We must understand what Christ has to say about the act of adultery, fornication or prostitution; Our Lord himself shows how the sin of adultery or fornication often begins in our thoughts, the point at which we lose the battle is in our hearts or minds when we consent to committing such actions.

Matthew 15; 18-20 But the things that come from out of the heart these are the things that make a person ritually unclean. For from his heart come the evil ideas which lead him to kill, commit adultery and do other immoral things.; to rob, lie, and slander others. These are the things that make a person unclean.

Fornication and adultery have led to a further breakdown of the family structure as more and more children are born to unwed mothers who become single parents. The structure of the family is vital for successful child rearing. Fortunately many grandparents and other relatives and friends fill the void in the family structure where necessary, we should be eternally grateful to those who do this. There is no doubt that the support of family or friends is required to provide the emotional, social, financial and educational needs involved in child rearing. In situations where a parent is single, provided there is no danger to the child, both parents and other family members should strive to make themselves available to provide the necessary family structure for successful child rearing.

If we live in sin, as long as we admit our faults, give up our sinful way of life, show true contrition and desire not to sin again, the Lord is willing to forgive us. This is precisely why Christ gave his life for us, because we are sinners and he wishes for us to gain eternal life. If Christ was willing to give up his life then we also must be willing to give up the flesh and all its desires that lead us to sin, we must live in the spirit as children of God. Christ eagerly awaits our return with open arms.

John 8; 4- "Teacher, they said to Jesus, 'this woman was caught in the very act of committing adultery. In our Law, Moses commanded that such a woman must be stoned to death, now what do you say? "Whichever one of you has committed no sin may throw the first stone at her' .He straightened up and said to her, 'Where are they, Is there no one left to condemn you?', .'No one sir', she answered. 'Well then' Jesus said, 'I do not condemn you either. Go, but do not sin again.'

Jesus Christ gives only one instruction as he forgives us our sin; "Do not sin again", connoting that if we are truly sorry and wish to be restored to life in the spirit, then we must intend not to sin again, Christ is indeed merciful and ever ready to forgive us. As we strive to die to our flesh and rise to life in the Holy Spirit we must remember that adultery and fornication are not in keeping with life in the Spirit.

CHAPTER TWENTY ONE

Pornography

Pornography often abbreviated 'Porn' is the explicit portrayal of sexual subject matter for the purpose of sexual gratification. Pornography includes images in books, magazines, photos, internet, video or film that range from nude images to other forms of sensual posture or actions to images of the act of sexual intercourse. Individuals indulge themselves with viewing these images so as to arouse themselves sexually. The intent in indulging in pornography is sexual gratification of some sort often culminating in the experience of an orgasm. As with most sins against the body, the question becomes 'Who is brought to harm if I indulge myself with these images and ultimately experience gratification of some sort, after all it is my body and I have hurt no one'.

Though these images may be derived from persons consenting to produce them often times the individuals displayed in this way are unwilling, in the cases of minors being abused they are obviously being exploited. The consenting subject when an adult is often willing to portray themselves in this way for a price or some other form of gain. The consumer of these materials often has no idea how these materials were acquired; willingly or forcefully however, the fact that we provide a market for these images means that these images will continue to be produced hence we encourage the perpetrators who produce this material. If we recognize the fact that the body is a temple of the Lord then we must also respect the body and not subject it to be used for such immoral acts as pornography. By indulging in these images we have consciously deciding not to guard our sense of sight or hearing and hence allow these images to influence our spirit mind. By repeatedly partaking in this indulgence we silence our conscience and can become addicted to this indulgence. We must guard our senses, guard our minds and fill ourselves only with images that are uplifting to the spirit. Anyone deriving sexual gratification from an individual other than a spouse is fornicating and this is not acceptable. If we live a life of discipline and diligence then we must strive to bring the body under control by the spirit rather than be ruled by emotions and the desires of the flesh.

If we agree that every time we sin against our body we give the spirit of lust access to our hearts and minds then we understand why we must not partake in such an activity as pornography. We must let our conscience which is the spirit within us speak to our hearts. If an act causes you to be ashamed then understand that the feeling of shame is the spirit speaking, and telling you not to partake in such activities. This sense of shame can lead to depression, aggression, anger, and the abuse of women or children. All arising from our loss of self-worth, a sense of self degradation that we feel for partaking in an act that we are ashamed of. If we have already judged ourselves, then we do not need to wait for the Lord to judge us in the matter of pornography. Let us make our sensual desires and activities acceptable and pleasing in the eyes of God, by indulging only with our married partner. I will only mention child pornography to remind us that sins against the innocent ones are unacceptable and even more grievous. Obviously any child whose images are sexually explicit is being abused; taken advantage of, unwilling, forced or knows no better and is being exploited. Any adult indulging in these images must absolutely understand that such acts are unforgivable and seek to alert the necessary authorities to ensure that this evil act does not continue.

Adolescents often indulge themselves in pornography and masturbation as they seek to explore their sensuality, but as they indulge themselves repeatedly they silence the spirit within themselves and awaken impulses that they desire to indulge. We must guard our senses and understand how indulging in pornography separates us from our Lord and the church which is the body of Christ. As children of the one true God we must be ever ready to give up the desires of the flesh and seek to walk in the Lord's precepts as he awaits us with open arms, each and every day, ever willing to forgive us and welcome us back into his fold. We must not forget to guard our eyes and only indulge in viewing images that are spiritually uplifting as indulging in pornography is not in keeping with life in the spirit of our Lord.

Matt 9: 47 - And if your eyes cause you to lose your faith, take it out! It is better for you to enter the kingdom of God with only one eye that to keep both eyes and be thrown into hell.

CHAPTER TWENTY TWO

Homosexuality

Homosexuality is sexual attraction and intercourse between individuals of the same gender.

The question of homosexuality and whether it is acceptable when we live in the spirit of Christ as Christians has led to heated debates in recent time. There is no question of whether sexual intercourse outside marriage is acceptable in the Christian faith hence this debate should not arise at all. Marriage according to our Christian faith is a union of a man and his wife. Individuals who are homosexual but have chosen to refrain from indulging their desires have given up the flesh and are living in the spirit of Christ. According to our Christian faith the only sensual desire that is acceptable and should be indulged is that of a husband and wife for each other.

Ephesians 5:31 "Therefore a man shall leave his father and mother and hold fast to his wife, and the two shall become one flesh.

As same gender marriage becomes the law in certain states, the question then becomes 'Is homosexual intercourse an adulterous act in states where same gender individuals are legally married by the state?' There is no doubt that the Lord wishes us to obey the law of the land, however, only in as much as it is in keeping with God's word. Same gender marriage is not acceptable anywhere in God's word, when Christ referred to marriage he always referred to marriage as union between a man and woman. In certain states same gender marriage is within the law but this only refers to the law of the state and is not referring to the law of God's word.

As Christians we can liken ourselves to travelers on a train, we earn a free ticket at the Departure station called 'Faith" once you profess a true faith in Christ Jesus; that he died on the cross for your salvation, that he resurrected from the dead, and that Christ's crucifixion earns us the grace to live according to God's purpose. All the faithful are given a free ticket no cancellation fees, no re-booking fees, no expiration date, valid from date of procurement and allowed to embark on this journey of life as Christians, but this is only the beginning of the journey that leads to eternal life.

Our first stop is at the station called 'Baptism unto Repentance', at this station all are called to acknowledge our sinful nature, confess of our sin and repent with the true intent to sin no more, at this station we receive the Baptism unto Repentance and are washed free of original sin. Some Christians depart from the train at the Repentance Station, because though we know the truth and understand the message of salvation, we refuse to repent of our sinful nature, we would rather live in sin and face the consequences of death rather than repent of our sin and continue on our journey to eternal life.

The next station is called 'Baptism unto death and the Gift of the Holy Spirit', for if we acknowledge a risen Christ, repent of our sins and are prepared to die to self, the Lord will grant us his grace which earns us eternal life. Our Lord is ever willing to provide us his grace by the Holy Spirit and after this station, sin no longer has power over us.

We must be willing to give up all we have and are to earn God's kingdom, much like the merchant did to earn the pearl of esteemed value in Matthew 14: 45-46 "Again, the kingdom of heaven is like a merchant looking for fine pearls. When he found one of great value, he went away and sold everything he had and bought it.

To receive our ultimate goal eternal life which awaits us at the final station, we must give up all that we possess including ourselves to death so that we may earn the ultimate gift 'eternal life'. If we cannot give up our flesh in death then we cannot rise to a new life in the Spirit, many believers go away sad at this station much like the rich man in Matthew 19; 21- 22 Jesus answered, "If you want to be perfect, go, sell your possessions and give to the poor, and you will have treasure in heaven. Then come, follow me." When the young man heard this, he went away sad, because he had great wealth.

There are several other stations called, The Word, Prayer, The Body and Blood of Christ, Forgiveness, Love; Works of Mercy, Love; Works of Faith, and the final destination is called Eternal Life. Unfortunately, many Christians get off at various stations before we reach the final destination.

Any Christian that chooses to live in sin rather than confess and repent got off at the second station. Those who refused to die to the flesh and rise to a new life in the spirit of Christ got off at the third station. Christ in his mercy has put a no re-booking, no cancellation fee, no expiration date on our ticket from our departure station, which means that we may present out ticket stub and get back on at the station we got off any time we choose, all that is required is our free will to accept the teachings at each station. If we have a faith that is true then we must die to the flesh and its needs and live according to God's purpose, once we give up our life of sin in true repentance we are welcome back on the train and once we receive the gift of the Holy Spirit and the grace that he brings us so that we may live according to our Lord's purpose and not our own we are assured of a journey that will earn us the crowning glory of 'Eternal Life' at our final destination.

As followers of Christ we must listen contemplatively to his answer when the young rich man asked him what to do to inherit eternal life.

Matthew 19; 16- 22 And behold a man came up to him, saying, "Teacher what good deed must I do to have inherit eternal life?" And he said to him, "Why do you ask me what is good? There is only one who is good. If you would enter life, keep the commandments." He said to him, "Which ones?" And Jesus said, "You shall not murder, You shall not commit adultery, You shall not steal, You shall not bear false witness, Honor your father and mother, and, You shall love your neighbor as yourself." The young man said to him all these I have kept. What do I still lack? Jesus said to him, "If you would be perfect, go, sell what you possess and give to the poor and you will have treasure in haven, and come, follow me."

When the young man heard this he went away sorrowful, for he had great possessions.

The rich young man enquired what a life in the Spirit that would culminate in eternal life entailed. There is no doubt that a life in the Spirit begins with obedience to his commands and the worship of our Lord then the love of our neighbor which we exhibit through our works of mercy, compassion and thoughtfulness as well as giving up the selfish desires of our heart such as jealousy, envy, pride and greed. The rich man appeared to have done all this and seemed willing to do even more. Then the question of sacrifice comes into play, give up all you are and have to surrender your entire life to worshiping the Lord. We also are required to give up all the indulgences of the flesh including adultery, fornication, pornography, homosexuality the choice is ours to make freely. If we refuse to sacrifice the selfish desires of the flesh then we also will go away sad like the rich young man. It is the grace of the Holy Spirit that transforms us from weak to strong so that we are enabled to give up the selfish desires of the flesh. We are all called to surrender, die to the flesh and receive the Holy Spirit of transformation as faithful children of God.

Peter's vision reassures us that whichever lifestyle we identify with, the Lord is ever willing to welcome us all into his fold and transform us with his Spirit. It is his Spirit that makes us worthy in his sight. Acts 10;10-14, 16, 34 And he became hungry and wanted something to eat, but while they were preparing it, he fell into a trance and saw the heavens opened and something like a great sheet descending, being let down by its four corners upon the earth. In it were all kinds of animals and reptiles and birds of the air. And there came a voice to him: "Rise, Peter; kill and eat." But

Peter said, "By no means, Lord; for I have never eaten anything that is common or unclean." This happened three times and, and the thing was taken up at once to heaven. So Peter opened his mouth and said: "Truly I understand that God shows no partiality, but in every nation anyone who fears him and does what is right is acceptable to him.

The Lord revealed a vision to Simon Peter at a time when he doubted that the salvation of Christ was for all people. As a Jew, Simon Peter believed that the circumcised Jews were the chosen, worthy and favored people of God to whom salvation was to come. The vision of the white sheet with all animals came to Simon Peter at a time when he would have been convinced that the message of salvation he shared was for the Jews alone and not the Gentiles. The voice of the Lord saying "kill and eat", confirming that all animals can be considered clean if they are created by the Lord was a revelation that set Simon Peter on his way to bringing the message of salvation to the Gentiles. There is no doubt that this vision of Simon Peter is as a valid today as it was at the time he received it; All men are created equal, all are called, all are worthy and are God's chosen people; homosexual, adulterer, married, single, we are all called to the foot of the cross that we may receive the transformation that only Christ and the Holy spirit can bring us. We must not allow the needs of the flesh cause us to reject the salvation that is ours for the claiming. We must answer the call to salvation with a "Here I am" as Abraham, Moses, Samuel, Isaiah, Ananias and all the Lord's disciples did in Genesis 22:11, Exodus 3:4, 1 Samuel 3, Isaiah 6:8, and Acts 9:10,

All of us are called, no one should doubt it and it is precisely for this reason that Christ died, so that all sinners may receive salvation. As we answer the call and present ourselves at the foot of the cross, we must be prepared to die with Christ to the flesh and its needs. We must give up all the needs and wants of the flesh that separate us from Christ and allow the Holy Spirit to transform us by his grace.

Children, except for in cases of sexual abuse of a child often have no idea of their sexual orientation. What is considered normal for them if often based on their personal observations of their environment, as well as through interaction with their community, boys want to be like their fathers while girls want to be like their mothers. This is why it is essential that we strive to nurture the family unit. As long as parents are responsible and not abusive, children must bond with their parents as this relationship serves to nurture them for their role as parents in the future. During the pre-teen years and adolescence some individuals become more aware of their sensuality and begin to experiment. Affection between individuals in pre-teen years is often between members of the same sex as well as individuals of the opposite sex. In the event that isolation occurs, individuals may begin to experiment with sensual behavior often not involving sexual intercourse. This is a crucial time spiritual direction and open communication must be provided by parents and the church. Boundaries that will enable us live in accordance with the Spirit of Christ must be established.

As with all sins against the body, the feeling of shame we feel for committing sinful acts should be regarded as the Spirit of God speaking to us in our conscience. If we repeatedly refuse to listen to the Spirit and instead justify our actions in our thoughts, individuals who are homosexual may at this point now make their inclination public, known as; coming out of the closet. Closet because they have been homosexual in secret; have not made their inclinations known to family or friends who they feel may judge them in a negative light if they make their feelings on intentions known. Coming out of the closet however unfortunately may also indicate that an individual has silenced his conscience and is no longer in a state of struggle with the choice of homosexuality. The Lord has written his laws in our hearts and mind; we must not silence our conscience which is the Spirit of God speaking to us in our hearts. It is not for me or any individual to judge the homosexual life style, each individual must listen to the Spirit of God within him speak and come to his or her own personal choice, by his or her own free will.

1 Cor 6: 9-11 Or do you not know that the unrighteous will not inherit the kingdom of God? Do not be deceived; neither the sexually immoral, nor idolaters, nor adulterers, nor men who practice homosexuality, nor thieves, nor the greedy, nor drunkards, nor revilers, nor swindlers will inherit the kingdom of God. And such were some of you. But you were washed, you were sanctified, you were justified in the name of the Lord Jesus Christ and by the Spirit of our God.

St.Paul in this verse to the Corinthians recognizes that many of Christ's followers had indulged the flesh and its desires before they became faithful followers, once Christ Jesus and the Holy Spirit transform us, we are put right with God and no longer choose to indulge the flesh but rather die to the flesh and live a life that is now dedicated to life in the Spirit of God. As children of the Spirit, we must give up the lusts of the flesh that are not in keeping with a life in the Spirit of God.

Christ awaits us patiently with open arms, to return to his fold each time we come off the train. Christ weeps because he continues to wait for us with open arms yet we allow our lack of faith, love and hope stand in the path of our salvation. By human strength it is impossible to give up our needs and die to the flesh but by the Lord's grace his Spirit empowers us and makes the impossible possible.

Our hope as Christians is that all believers will be united in our Father's kingdom at the end of time and our prayer is that on this earth, all will answer the call to salvation and give up the desires of the flesh that obstruct the path of our answer to the call of salvation like the eunuch in Matthew 19;12 For there are eunuchs who were born that way, and there are eunuchs who have been made eunuch's by others – and there are those who choose to live like eunuchs for the sake of the kingdom of heaven. The one who can accept this should accept it."

The Lord invites all homosexuals, adulterers and those who live in sin to profess their faith and stand at the foot of his cross so that as they die to the flesh with all its desires and give up their needs, the Holy Spirit will transform them to a new life in the Spirit where sin no longer has power over them so that we all may sit and dine at the table of the Lord now and at the end of time.

CHAPTER TWENTY THREE

Abortion

• An abortion is the termination of a pregnancy by the removal or expulsion from the uterus of a fetus.

• In a spontaneous abortion, this is not purposely performed the fetus or embryo undergoes spontaneous expulsion before it is viable. A spontaneous abortion is often referred to as a miscarriage and is not purposeful or planned.

• In an induced abortion the act of abortion is purposely performed for varying reasons ranging from unplanned pregnancy to health risks or fetal abnormalities.

Hence forth when we refer to abortion, we will take this to mean an induced or purposeful abortion. Abortion goes against everything we stand for as Christians. Our Lord instructed us thus in the book of Exodus 22:25 "When men strive together and hit a pregnant woman, so that her children come out, but there is no harm, the one who hit her shall surely be fined, as the woman's husband shall impose on him, and he shall pay as the judges determine. But if there is harm you shall pay life for life, eye for eye, tooth for tooth, hand for hand, foot for foot, burn for burn, stripe for stripe."

It is even more reprehensible that the life that we take in an abortion is an innocent one that has done us no harm, as in committing any harm against an innocent child, the consequences are grave.

Mark 9:42-" If anyone causes one of these little ones- those who believe in me to stumble, it would be better for them if a large millstone were hung around their neck and they were thrown into the sea".

The sin of abortion is not just against one's body but against the most innocent of lives, an unborn child. This child also is a member of Christ's body that is yet to be viable and unable to survive without the life giving Spirit of its mother. Children are dependent on their parents; we need to feed them, care for them, and nurture them. Even more so as the unborn child is dependent on its mother as this life cannot survive without a mother's love and life giving spirit. The unborn child is a portion of father and mother yet entirely dependent on its mother for life and is the closest comparison we can make to the union of Christ with his Father and the Holy Spirit, three separate beings yet one. These separate relationships illustrate how the Spirit of Christ binds us together as one. A mother conceived with child is an image of glory and honor, an evidence of man's role in the heavenly act of pro-creation. Perhaps our Lord could have created man through a different process, but he chose to give us this glory as mere women, that only through our co-operation world he create any human-being of flesh. There is no doubt that a woman conceived with child displays a reflection of God's love for the church as she alone can bring the role of man in creation to its complete fruition. The Lord has loved us so much and trusted us so much that he has allowed us to share with him in the sacred gift of creation. The Lord fills a female with compassion and a true love that causes her to carry an unborn child to term and bring it into the world. A woman filled with true love and compassion must go against everything within her being; body, spirit and mind to terminate a pregnancy. Why would we break this bond of divine love, for our own selfish reasons, absolutely against the example given us when Christ gave his life on the cross for our salvation. The love of Christ for man when he gave up his life for the redemption of his chosen people the church, is a true demonstration of absolute sacrifice and love. A mother terminating the life of her child, her very own flesh and blood is absolutely against the example Christ gave us on the cross, giving his life for us. Christ did not choose the easy way out, he did not deny us even as he lay bleeding on the cross. The love Christ has for his church must be mirrored by a mother's love for her unborn child. Every time we justify an abortion, we put another nail in Christ's palm, we put another spear in his side, we crucify him again. Abortion is such a great sin against our body, against Christ, against the body of Christ, against the Love that we are known for as Christians, because it is a sin against the innocent unborn that belong to Christ.

Let us examine how abortion occurs so as to understand how to best prevent it. Pregnancy occurs through sexual intercourse, there is no rule that says that sexual intercourse is solely for procreation but as with all activities that bring us pleasure we must understand that we must indulge in a responsible manner and this act is permissible only if participating partners are married. If indulging involves breaking God's word then the choice becomes, do I satisfy my own bodily desires or obey the Holy Spirit. The answer is undoubtedly that we obey our Lord's will that sexual intercourse should only occur between consensual married individuals. We often justify the sin of abortion by convincing ourselves that we are sinners and not righteous hence insinuating that a sin by a sinner need not be accounted for before God as we are already given our soul up to final damnation. True, our Lord is ever willing to forgive us when we fall to sins of the flesh however when this sin is not just against our body but against an unborn child of God, we indeed have put a heavy weight around our neck. Adultery or fornication is a sin of our flesh alone, while abortion is a sin against our own flesh as well as the flesh of an unborn child. Married mothers also commit abortion so this act is not reserved for fetal life conceived through adultery or fornication. After a child is conceived a mother might justify this evil act by reasoning such as; she is unable to provide for her child, she is embarrassed that her sin of fornication will now be discovered by an obvious pregnancy, she is unwed and not willing to live her life as a single mother, she feels she is not financially able, she feels this unborn child will prevent her from securing an education or a career. All imaginable reasons for an abortion are selfish and based on the mother putting herself first. Fathers are often involved in this decision but ultimately except she is held down and her child forcefully removed from her, a mother's ultimate consent is required for this abhorrent act to occur. In certain instances where a genetic defect or malformation not compatible with life is present in a fetus we must remember that our Lord alone gives life and he alone has the right to take it, this is a tough situation and we must seek guidance from our Pastor, Priest or spiritual director. Mother connotes a loving, caring, compassionate, thoughtful individual, willing to put the life of her unborn child before her own life, just as Mary put Christ first, just as Christ put us first, sacrificing himself for our salvation. An unborn child may be conceived as a result of an act of lust performed in the heat of the moment once this act has occurred and a mother is conceived with child, what do we then do in this situation. Let us take a minute to contemplate Mary's response to her unplanned conception, the angel Gabriel tells Mary in Luke 1;30; Don't be afraid Mary, God has been gracious to you. You will become pregnant and give birth to a son, and you will name him Jesus.

Mary the mother of Christ was a single unwed mother, and is now conceived by the Holy Spirit, pregnant and unwed. Her response was 'Behold the handmaid of the Lord; be it unto me according to thy word." Luke 1; 38 This is a resounding example to all mothers in a similar situation, saying yes to the Lord's will and no to the flesh means giving an unborn child the chance of life. If Mary had said no to the Lord and destroyed the child within her, we would have had no hope of salvation. If we have no wish or means to provide for a child then we must consider all our options such as adoption or the support of family and the church. We must take all precautions to abstain from pre-marital sex because once a child is conceived we are the parent and our goal should be to protect this child, not to destroy its life but to nurture it. Any option other than this is not in keeping with life in the Spirit of Christ.

Mary's act of true obedience gives evidence of the faith and love that she had for our Lord. She gave up her inhibitions of the flesh in this statement and submitted to God's will perfectly and totally. Each time we say no to a child conceived within us we cause the devil to rejoice as we reject the salvation that Christ has gained for us, we are jeering at Christ with the crowd and screaming with the crowd, rejecting our Lord and savior as we say with the crowd crucify him, crucify him', for if we would not crucify an innocent Christ, why would we crucify an innocent unborn child.

There is no sin that can separate us from Christ's love for us, he died for this very purpose that no sin should be great enough to separate us from our salvation. All that is left is that we understand how abortion is a sin against the most innocent of God's creation and against our Lord himself. For those who carry out abortions and those who have allowed their un-born child be aborted or are considering such an act, the time is now to repent of our ways and return to our Father's house, much like the prodigal son did. The time is now to make our faith not just a thought but an action in obedience to God's will. The choice is ours, we must understand the magnitude of the act of abortion and if we have committed such an act we must confess unto our Lord with true contrition and repent with the true intent not to sin again. The Lord is ever ready to forgive us and send us his Holy Spirit to strengthen us if we intend never to sin again. As we strive to live in the Spirit of God we must understand as children of God that abortion is not in keeping with life in the Spirit.

CHAPTER TWENTY FOUR

Divorce

In our day and age divorce has become an act performed by Christians and non-Christians. Divorce and remarriage are allowed by the civil law which is the law of the land but divorce and remarriage are not always allowed by the Law of our Lord as in the word of God.

If we truly believe in the word of God then we must understand that in marriage two separate beings of flesh and spirit become one. There are only a few instances when separate individuals are one in the spirit such as; Christ and the church, God the Father, God the son and God the Holy Spirit are one in the Holy Trinity, all baptized Christians are one in the Spirit of Christ. This union of man and wife, is a true lasting union in the Spirit and the married couple are permitted to come together as one in the physical through sexual intercourse. Marriage is a union that is made possible by the Spirit of God, we cannot be one in the Spirit if we do not present ourselves in his presence and ask that the Spirit of God bind us together as one. As Christians it is possible to marry in the presence of the court but it is also necessary to present oneself for marriage before the Holy Spirit and the church in the presence of our Lord.

Christ himself said in Mark 10:9 "What therefore God has joined together, let not man separate." Hence, this should be a warning to any person that comes between a man and his wife, and causes them to divorce. Divorce is a sin against our body not in the flesh but in the Spirit hence when we commit divorce, we have sinned against the Spirit of the Lord that binds both individuals together as one.

It is a general belief that all married couples come to a union of spirit and flesh, as a result of the great love they mutually share. For those who have not married out of love they will be more likely to divorce because lust soon passes and we become disillusioned with a partner we do not truly love. True love is patient, kind, thoughtful, considerate, generous, compassionate, and never ending, every couple needs to understand this. Once we become intolerant, impatient, selfish, angry, we quickly become disillusioned with marriage. Adultery or any other sin against the body will also cause us to be disillusioned with our marriage because we are now consciously satisfying our bodily desires from another source and our spouse who is now no longer considered desirable suddenly becomes expendable.

To prevent divorce, communication is the key, we must not let anger or hatred brew within our hearts because it takes up the room of the love within our hearts. Whatever the situation, it is important the desire to save the marriage is mutual and a couple has to strive to forgive each other and begin the relationship anew.

Each day is an opportunity to resolve our conflict or differences and begin anew.

The home of a married couple should be a place of love, a mirror of the love the Lord has for Christ, Christ has for the Church, and we as the body of Christ have for Christ and for each other. Once we allow the love in our homes to be extinguished, we make room for hate and evil thoughts and desires in our heart to thrive, contempt will always thrives where there is darkness and turmoil. Each married person must understand the meaning of the word love as a term between married individuals. To do this, they must first understand the love that Christ has for us as sinners, a love that meant he was ready to give his life that we may live, this is true love. If our love for each other only in as much as we act in accordance with each other's personal needs and desires then this is not true love. True love means we are often willing to sacrifice our personal needs and desires for the fulfillment of the needs of a spouse. As married individuals we have to understand that each individual has separate needs and wants, true love means trying to understand these needs and meeting them in so far as they are in keeping with our Lord's purpose. True love is unconditional, everlasting, enduring and mutual meaning that each partner is often ready to make sacrifices for the other, true love is never one sided.

Christ offered himself as a holy sacrifice out of the love he has for us, so also should a married couple be willing to offer sacrifices out of the love they have for each other. The love of a married couple should mirror the love of Christ for his church which is indeed, ever selfless and all sacrificing. Each time we undergo divorce, we cause pain to our very selves, the body of Christ, his church and Christ himself. We act against the greatest of all commandments; To Love our Lord our God with all our hearts and to love our neighbor or spouse as ourselves. Loss of financial security, pressures at work, different religious beliefs or faith, different cultures, wants or desires unfulfilled, adultery and other sins against the body can put stress on a marriage. As a couple we must strive to support each other both financially, spiritually emotionally and physically. We must understand that the Lord has given us a helper in a spouse and, we must have faith in the Lord that he will provide for our needs even as we provide education, career training or self-development as required to a spouse so that the family is well provided for regardless of circumstances. Conflict will always arise in every marriage and we should always seek guidance from the word of God as well as from our spiritual guides or counsellors where necessary as we seek to hear the voice of God minister to us in our times of struggle.

In certain circumstances, family members or friends might interfere in a marriage; this could be detrimental to a marriage if the interference is destructive. We must immediately recognize this interference as negative and make moves to prevent such further interference. In situations where a family member provides the insight or spiritual support that helps us cope with stress in a relationship, we can accept their help in as much as it uplifts us in the spirit.

The Lord has told us clearly what his position is on divorce in several verses in his holy word. 1 Cor7: 10 For married people, I have a command which is not my own but the Lord's; a wife must not leave her husband, but if she does, she must remain single or else be reconciled to her husband, and a husband must not divorce his wife.

Matt 19: 3 Some Pharisees came to him and tried to trap him by asking. 'Does our law allow a man to divorce his wife, for whatever reason he wishes?' Jesus answered haven't you read the scripture that says that in the beginning the creator made people male and female? And God said for this reason a man will leave his father and mother and unite with his wife, and the two will become one. So they are no longer two but one. Man must not separate then, what God has joined together.

Jesus says in Matthew 19;9 I tell you then that any man who divorces his wife for any course other than her unfaithfulness commits adultery, if he marries some other woman.

Only in certain circumstances such as adultery does Christ permit this act of divorce, if a partner is willing to desist from such an act as adultery, and is willing to receive counseling, learn new ways to correct past errors then it may be in the heart of the offended spouse to forgive and be reconciled. The Lord does also instruct that once divorced one must not remarry, save for the reason of an adulterous wife in which case we may remarry, this may seem harsh on this heavenly earth but if we have true faith and believe that the world to come is where we will receive our eternal glory then we surely must strive to obey all of God's word. Christ understood that certain circumstances may necessitate divorce, he only mentioned adultery as far as is recorded in the word of God.

In any situation that puts a spouse at risk of spousal abuse or physical injury or harm, it is imperative that one remove one's self from such a relationship and seek a safe haven for self and children. Where an offending spouse is willing to seek help and a true conversion then reconciliation may remain a possibility but in a case where the offending spouse has a heart that remains hardened and a spirit that remains of the flesh hence seeks no repentance or conversion, then a separation or divorce is often the only solution that ensures the safety of the abused spouse and children.

We must judge no one, divorce is a very personal decision that should not be considered lightly, where there is room for conversion and reconciliation in a safe environment this should always be our foremost option. We should seek help from pastors and priests, counselors and mental health professionals that can lead us to healing and reconciliation before we seek a permanent dissolution of marriage.

As with all sins of the flesh, divorce is not in keeping with a life in the spirit so we must not allow divorce to separate us from the great love that our Lord has for us. Instead let us seek for counseling and reconciliation where this is safe and possible. We must never take this permanent step without seeking advice and counsel from Spirit filled family members as well as Pastors and Priest. In all circumstance we must allow the spirit of God minister to us through his word and our Spirit filled counsel, for the Spirit can heal that which is broken, as children of God we must work to preserve our marriages by communication, prayer, tolerance and sacrifice in all circumstances.

CHAPTER TWENTY FIVE

Drug Abuse

The abuse of a drug can be defined as the use of a drug of abuse or mind altering substances for the sole purpose of producing a mind altering sensation, popularly known as being high. In this state of mind the sense of judgment is altered. Once the sense of judgment is impaired then the ability to determine a state of sin is impaired. In such a state of gone might rationalize a sinful act as being an acceptable act. Unfortunately as with all drugs of abuse, one soon requires an increased quantity of a drug to produce a mind altering sensation and with repeated use of the drug becomes addicted to a drug of abuse; meaning that they desperately seek this sense of 'a high' at all costs otherwise they begin to experience a withdrawal or some form of physical impairment after being deprived of the drug for a prolonged period. The sense of withdrawal further drives the need to acquire a drug of abuse, hence the vicious cycle; use, abuse, addiction, sin against the body, high, withdrawal, use, abuse, sin against others and the cycle continues.

Drugs commonly abused include alcohol, opiates; such as codeine, morphine, heroine, stimulants such as amphetamines, cocaine, speed and hallucinogens such as marijuana, PCP; phencyclidine.

Drug abuse is a sin of the flesh for the fact that it results in the loss of the voice of the Holy Spirit within us which is our conscience. A drug of abuse also alters our sense of judgment and insight making such reprehensible acts as; pornography, adultery, fornication, homosexuality, child abuse, and prostitution acceptable to us. An individual under the influence of a drug of abuse is also more likely to commit other crimes such as; rape, murder, assault and theft because they lose all sense of judgment and for the purpose of acquiring some form of monetary gain to aid them in acquiring the substance to which they are addicted. Individuals under the influence of drugs silence the Holy Spirit within them and once they lose their sense of judgment and insight often have no regard for the law of God or the law of the land. Drug abusers often become sociopaths, due to losing the voice of the Holy Spirit within them and may go on to commit reprehensible crime.

Let us analyze the sequence of events as drug abuse leads to sin against the body. In certain instances drugs abused are initially prescribed legitimately for a genuine medical condition such as pain. Drugs of abuse are also often introduced initially for social or recreational use, it may seem like the in thing to use alcohol and other illicit substances especially to an impressionable adolescent. Sometimes due to peer pressure an individual might decide to experiment or try out alcohol or a drug of abuse. Another reason adolescents experiment is plain inquisitiveness, such a person might want to experience the feeling of a high or a drunken stupor first hand. If an individual wants to be perceived as cool such a person might begin to experiment with drugs as a recreational habit. Adolescents often refer to the altered sensorium, loss of inhibition and judgment that comes from consuming alcohol as being buzzed, in his state an individual has lost the voice of the Holy Spirit within and will seek to fulfill the desires of the flesh even when they are against the will of the Spirit.

Inquisitiveness and experimenting is opening the door to drug addiction and walking through it. One has to understand the recrimination of such actions. Drugs of abuse stimulate certain receptors in the portion of the brain that cause a sensation of drowsiness, a feeling of wellbeing, a sense of hyper-alertness or stimulation, a feeling of pleasure, or an overwhelming sense of wellbeing often described as a high, the sensation experienced depends on the drug used and the portion of the brain in which it stimulates receptors.

At some point the use of the drug becomes primarily for the purpose of a 'high' or mind altered state rather than for genuine pain or just acting cool. This is the point to recognize that a person is addicted, a physical sign of addiction might be; requiring increased quantities of these illicit substances to achieve the same sensation or to feel a high, the presence of withdrawal symptoms once an individual fails to consume a drug for a period of time. The question then becomes what alternatives do we have, it might be possible to request medications that do not have mind altering properties, for genuine pain. It might be possible to find a cure for the underlying condition causing pain such as physiotherapy for back pain. Another option to treat an underlying condition such as stress or pain might be to try other homeopathic means or proven methods such as acupuncture or yoga. It is necessary to seek help from qualified health professionals and enter a drug abuse rehabilitation and counselling program if all self-help efforts have failed. These and other options may need to be discussed with a medical provider.

Inquisitiveness and experimenting is often the first stage of an addiction, seeking a high and experiencing the withdrawal that follows is the next stage. Once an individual repeatedly strives to experience a high he is addicted to the illicit substance sought. An individual that cannot abstain from use of a drug for a prolonged period and begins to experience withdrawal symptoms which further fuel the craving for the drug is now dependent on this drug of abuse. Once an individual is dependent on a drug of abuse they become desperate and are often prepared to obtain these drugs of abuse through unsavory means.

It is important that as individuals we understand the consequences of our actions before we commit such actions as drug use. It is only in a truly informed state of mind that we can understand that the struggle or battle against addiction should begin simply at the thought of drug use even before experimenting. By the stage of addiction the battle has already been lost; professional help and spiritual intervention is useful at all stages of drug abuse but necessary at the stage of addiction. We must not forget our role as God's temple and must strive to remain subject to the Spirit of God rather than to illicit drugs that cause us to be slaves of the flesh.

CHAPTER TWENTY SIX

Christ's Crucifixion

The crucifixion was our ultimate no to Christ, we rejected him, humiliated him, mocked him and hurt him physically when we scourged him and crowned him with thorns, and then we crucified him. Christ, who had only ever shown us love, yet we turned our backs on him and crucified him. As our Lord sees how those whom he had ever only shown love mock him and treat him with contempt he looks to his Father in heaven and says Matthew 27;46:' My Lord my God, why have you forsaken me.' He looks to his left and right and the two to be crucified with him stand for all men. One thief will repent and ask for mercy saying ' Jesus, remember me when you come into your kingdom." Luke 23:42. More like the laborer to arrive last at the field and receive the same wages as the first, the Lord as with all sinners always ready to forgive us and reconcile us to himself welcomed him into his kingdom that day when he said in Luke 23;43, "Truly I say to you, today you will be with me in Paradise.". The Lord did not become cynical, bitter, and vicious or begin to hate in the face of adversity .The other man to be crucified let cynicism and narcissism stand in the way of his salvation as he mocked Jesus saying in Luke 23;39 "Are you not the Christ,? Save yourself and us! Let us not allow pride and sin stand in the way of our salvation. If we do not repent of your sinful ways, believe and ask for salvation, then we alone are responsible for obstructing our own path to salvation.

May the Lord open our eyes to examine the sins of the flesh that we commit, knowingly or unknowingly that stands in the path of our salvation: be it envy, greed, pride, lust, hate, jealousy, discontent, pain, sickness, laziness, sloughtfulness, pornography, homosexuality, adultery, drugs of abuse, alcoholism or gluttony, let us take all this to our Lord and surely he will grant us the grace to overcome as we die to the flesh, so we also may share in eternal life with him at the end of time.

The worst part for me as Christ is crucified on the cross is not looking above, or around him, it is Christ looking down at the crowd for this is what must fill him with so much sorrow.

Where are his friends? Surely some were there hiding in the crowds, afraid to identify with him for fear of being crucified with him. They were perhaps, confused, upset, sad, and downcast, did they fully understand that Christ's death would earn us all salvation? Probably not so at this time, besides, if Christ's death was for the purpose of salvation, it makes it no easier to bear. I believe Christ sees each and every one of them as they are filled with fear, and perhaps just their presence brings him a little joy on the cross. Surely he is not alone, his friends are united with him in his sufferings and share his sorrow and pain. No one said a word in his defense, the Holy Spirit and Pentecost would be earned by the crucifixion so Christ was willing to make this great sacrifice. The Holy Spirit was available to man even prior to Pentecost,, but even more so after the crucifixion he made himself freely available to all men. This was all as it was meant to be, for only through his crucifixion would Christ earn us salvation. Christ had to bear the burden all on his own; he alone would bare the cross that would earn us salvation. There was no need for the Apostles to be crucified with Christ, their work to share the message of salvation was to be done later.

O loving Jesus, I see you on the cross alone. I know you understood the hearts of men, those you healed through your miracles, and with whom you shared your words of wisdom, were all full of fear, some were hiding far away, some mingled with the crowd, but not one came to your defense. Those you had loved, fed and provide for in their time of need, turned their backs on you. These were the ones that brought you sorrow on the cross as they turned their backs on you, jeered at you: physician heal yourself, healer heal thyself, king of the Jews save yourself. Those who had felt first-hand the healing power of your touch, heard the healing power of your word, known the healing power of your love and always surrounded and followed you as crowds now turned their backs on you. They persistently wanted to feed on your words, be healed by you, wanted to touch you and reach you. They who knew you, your sisters, brothers and friends that turned their backs against you must have caused you the most sorrow.

There were those in the crowd who never knew you, perhaps had never seen you, some had never known of you yet they delighted in your sorrow, even though you had never done them any harm. They now found joy in your pain and suffering, they stand for the sinful nature of man and for evil. We see how evil manifests himself in men that welcome him and make room for him in their hearts by selfishness, hate, anger, jealousy, greed, distrust and envy. These friends of yours and the crowds who were against you also brought you sorrow. People you had only shown love, were now filled with such hate towards you.

The crowds judged you and asked for you to be crucified, in exchange for a thief, Luke 23: 18-21 But they all cried out together, "away with this man and release to us Barabbas".- a man who had been thrown into prison for an insurrection started in the city and for murder. Pilate addressed them once more, desiring to release Jesus, but they kept shouting "Crucify him, crucify him"

Perhaps they had been incited by the teachers of the Law, the Pharisees and Sadducees, those hypocrites who were always quick to judge you, whose pride, wealth, knowledge, anger, envy and hatred stopped them from accepting you for who you were, the Son of God. They, who came to know the Law and know the word, yet the law and the word had no part in their hardened hearts. Those who claimed to believe but yet were blind to the truth. They in their pride, anger, jealousy and hatred wanted your death. They, who were in positions of authority and able to lead the crowd turned the crowds against you and paid Judas to betray you. They stood with glee and were glad as the crowds they incited, screamed crucify him, crucify him. See what anger, hate, wealth, jealousy, envy, and greed, can do. See why the rich in wealth are often poor in virtue, why they remain blind, deaf and dumb though they claim to be God's people. They will not receive salvation from the cross if they continue to allow their pride stand in the way of their salvation. May those in positions of authority use their influence wisely, whenever they incite the crowd to move in a certain direction, and may those in the crowds learn to make decisions based on their own personal experience rather than on what they are instructed to do by others.

We know know that man is made in God's likeness and that the spirit within us exists though we often seek to satisfy our flesh, our needs, our wants and our feelings. This is why you granted us your infinite mercy even in your sorrow and suffering on the cross you spoke to us the ultimate words of mercy "Father forgive them, for they know not what they do". May we all repent and ask forgiveness for our sins, may we also remember to forgive those who might have offended us as vengeance is not for us.

I thank the Lord for those in the crowd who were there, not there to jeer at you but to share your sorrow and pain, for I know this brought you some comfort. Your mother Mary, the disciple you loved John, Mary Magdalene the adulterous woman whom you saved from death by stoning, she repented to sin no more, and did not allow sins against the body separate her from you. May we follow the example of Mary Magdalene, as we confess and repent of the sins against the body we commit, and ask for the grace of your spirit, that we may sin no more. Mary Magdalene is the sole example at the foot of the cross to show us that sins against the body need not separate us from salvation. All we need to do is repent, and sin no more and you will welcome us. There were probably others, some women from Jerusalem, weeping, sharing your sorrow, showing no joy in your time of distress. These followers of yours bring me some joy, they were never too far from you as you carried the cross. They were not too far from you as you cried out in the last hour.Your brothers and sisters, those from your mother's house, your cousins, the other Apostles were not at the foot of the cross. But the few who were with brought you so much joy, gladness, peace, hope. May we also bring joy, gladness, peace and hope to our brothers and sisters who carry their cross in our presence. Open our eyes O Lord; that we may not be blind to the suffering of others.

Lord, you knew your work was done, your time had come. You knew, you had to drink this cup and be crucified. You alone, but those at the foot of the cross brought you even more strength. They showed their love for you in action with every step they took with you. Every prayer they said for you. You worried for your mother, even as you lay dying on the cross just as you worried for all widows and the widow of Nain when you said in Luke 7:16, 'who would provide for her?'

Even as you lay in pain, sorrow, dying, thirsting on the cross you made arrangements for one last widow your mother: and told John to provide for her as you told her to watch over John. "Mother behold your son, son behold your mother' John 19: 26-27; Giving us that special gift of Mary as the mother to all your friends that stand with you at the foot of your cross. May we forever love and honor your holy mother as you did, and may she continue to intercede on our behalf much like she did at that first miracle at the wedding at Cana. May we also understand that as we share in God's work we must always be ready to provide ourselves as helpers to all widows and orphans that we meet on our path of life.

You alone had to carry that cross till exhaustion then Simon of Cyrene was asked to help for they did not want you dead before you were crucified. You alone bore the pain and sorrow, what you suffered most was sorrow at the hardness of the hearts of men, at the greed jealousy and envy in the hearts of men. Sorrow at the joy they felt in your suffering, that the world would rejoice so much in your pain. Sorrow at how they taunted you, jeered at you, humiliated you, sorrow at their greed as they cast lots for your robes, sorrow at their blindness as their sins caused them not to see. You must have been filled with sorrow at the frenzy and excitement as the crowd gathered to send you to your death. This sorrow caused you to say the words "I thirst" in John 19:28. Yes, you thirst for all these lost souls that have chosen freely to follow the path of flesh, instead of the path of the Spirit that leads to salvation. You thirst as you see first-hand, the evil in man's heart, the hate within each of us, the joy we feel at another's downfall, you thirst at our anger, our lust, greed, envy and pride which stands in the way of our salvation. You thirst as we seem lost, like sheep without a shepherd with no one to lead us, simply because we refused to follow. You thirst, at our blindness, our deafness as we refuse to heed your words and yield to the Holy Spirit. You thirst because of your sorrow at the state of mankind.

You drank the wine from the hyssop to fulfill the words of scripture in Psalm 69:21 They gave me poison for my food, and for my thirst they gave me sour wine to drink.

At the end you said in John 19: 30 "it is finished"; you had fulfilled the word, you gave yourself freely as the final offering that would earn man salvation and bring him life. Your work was done.

Your last words in Luke 23: 46 " Father into your hands I commend your spirit", a contrast to your earlier lamentation: "My Lord, My God, why have you forsaken me"; you alone were the ultimate sacrifice, no one not even your father or angels could bare that burden with you. Perhaps you felt despair for a minute at the time of your earlier lamentation, at that time, the darkness that came in the heart made you feel desolate, alone, isolated, but as with all the trials you experienced, you overcame and finished your work. Even now as you passed knowing your work was done you committed your Spirit into your father's hands. May we also have that opportunity every day of our lives and at the minute of our death to commit our spirit into our father's hands. May the grace you earned us by your crucifixion, through our faith, truly bring us to re-birth in the Spirit and eternal life.

CHAPTER TWENTY SEVEN

Call to a New Life in the Spirit of Christ

In my own personal experience as a physician, I have personally witnessed several miracles of life being returned to the dead. In two of these incidents I was used as the Lord's instrument. I will mention these incidents only so as to further help us understand deeper the significance of rising from death to a new life.

The first incident was a neonate who while on a ventilator suddenly developed a tension pneumothorax, which is a sudden air leak from ruptured small airways that leak into the chest and can cause pressure that stops the heart. Her heart rate and oxygen saturation immediately started to drop and there was no time to get an X-ray to diagnose the possible cause of her sudden decompensation, this child was dying. While speaking to my neonatologist attending on the phone I turned out the lights, trans-illuminated the neonate's chest with a flash light, which caused a fluorescence on the side of the chest with the pneumothorax. I immediately inserted a wide bore needle through the chest wall and released the tension pneumothorax. This child's heart rate and oxygen saturation were immediately restored, within a few seconds her color returned and once my attending arrived, we went on to insert a chest tube.

The second incident was an infant with a high fever, who while receiving an injection suddenly stopped breathing and became unresponsive his parents and the nurse rushed with him into my room next door. I asked the mother to leave the room as she was panicked, his father remained while I told the nurse to get the resuscitation cart to resuscitate the child. As my nurse left the room the baby had started turning blue as he was not taking any spontaneous breaths, by the grace of the Holy Spirit I immediately knew that there was no time to wait for the resuscitation cart. I had to give mouth to mouth breaths immediately, by my third administered breath, this baby took a voluntary breath, his color soon returned and he cried so loud that when the nurse returned with the crash cart she could barely believe that this was the lifeless baby she had brought to me a few minutes ago. I can testify that the breath of the Spirit does give life.

The third incident was my own personal experience, after a road traffic accident in 2010 while on vacation in my home country Nigeria. I was found unconscious and unresponsive. My family had given me up for dead but while being transported to the hospital, I started to speak and move. I had sustained a concussion a minor un-displaced spine fracture and a femoral and hip fracture with dislocation. A few days later while being transported to an aircraft to bring me back to the United States, I again lapsed into unconsciousness and had to be resuscitated a second time then transferred back to the intensive care unit. I was unable to make the flight that day and I firmly believe that the Lord brought me back to life a second time.

These three incidents ministered to me personally and strengthened my faith and I hope they ministered to the family members and friends who witnessed these events. The parents and family members rejoiced that their children were eventually well enough to go home. The significance of this is that rising from the dead on its own as an action is an amazing event mostly to those who witness it. The amazement in itself soon fades and might even be forgotten. The act of 'rising from the dead' is only of value if it has caused us to experience the greatness of our Lord's glory and caused us to repent and return to Christ in true humility and faith. It is this faith that earns us the grace of the Holy Spirit within us that transforms us to be born of the Spirit. It is only if we come to experience this re-birth of the Holy Spirit that we can truly say that the rising from the dead we witnessed has transformed us. If we witness a 'rising from the dead' or any other miracle and are not transformed in the spirit, then the miracle though an amazing event in itself was in vain.

Mark 2;3-12 And they came, bringing to him a paralytic carried by four men. And when they could not get near him because of the crowd, they removed he roof above him, and when they had made an opening, they let down the bed on which the paralytic lay. And when Jesus saw their faith, he said to the paralytic, "Son your sins are forgiven". Now some of the scribes were sitting there, questioning in their hearts, "Why does this man speak like that? He is blaspheming! Who can forgive sins but God alone? And immediately Jesus, perceiving in his spirit that they thus questioned within themselves, said to them, "Why do you question these things within your hearts? Which is easier, to say to the paralytic, 'Your sins are forgiven,' or to say, 'Rise, take up your bed and walk'? But that you may know that the Son of Man has authority on earth to forgive sins' – he said to the paralytic - "I say to you, rise, pick up your bed, and go home." And he rose and immediately picked up his bed and went out before them all, so that they were all amazed and glorified God, saying, "We never saw anything like this!"

Christ came precisely for this that our faith might bring us the salvation that is a new life in his Spirit. We can only drink of this new life in the Spirit after we have been washed free of our sin in the water of repentance by our baptism. This re-birth to a new life in Christ after we die to sin and the flesh means we now exist as a new being in the Spirit of Christ. As people of flesh we are moved to amazement like the crowd was when we see healing in the physical, unfortunately the new life in the spirit that Christ gives us is not visual. Our Lord himself asks this question, 'Which is easier, to say to the paralytic, 'Your sins are forgiven,' or to say, 'Rise, take up your bed and walk'? Mathew 2;9.

As physical beings we tend to be amazed only by the miracles we can see in the physical, and we often fail to appreciate the miracles in the Spirit. Christ has come that we may receive the forgiveness of sin that can restore us to being children of God. After Adam sinned and caused death to our spirit it was Christ who came to give up his life and restore us to life in the spirit. Illness in as much as it brings us to humility can cause us to present ourselves to Christ, as much as we pray for a healing in the physical we must also have a desire for a healing in the Spirit otherwise we would have borne our cross in vain.

Luke7; 12-17 As he drew near to the gate of the town, behold, a man who had died was being carried out, the only son of his mother, and she was a widow, and a considerable crowd from the town was with her. And when the Lord saw her, he had compassion for her and said to her. "Do not weep." Then he came up and touched the bier, and the bearers stood still. And he said, "Young man, I say to you, arise." And the dead man sat up and began to speak, and Jesus gave him to his mother. Fear seized them all, and they glorified God, saying a great prophet has arisen among us!" and "God has visited his people!" And this resort about him spread through the whole of Judea and all the surrounding country.

The widow in the town of Nain was probably desolate and had lost all hope. First her husband had left her in death, now her only son had died, she was now alone in the world. Any mother would be distressed at the loss of a child, talk less of if it was an only child. The widow of Nain does not seem to have known Jesus Christ before this incident but there is no doubt in my mind that she had cried out to the Lord in her anguish. Jesus Christ came upon her and had compassion for her, it was this compassion that he had for her that caused him to bring her son back to life. The whole town saw the glory of God in this act and there is no doubt in my mind that many of these people became believers in Christ that very day. The raising to life of the widows son is another amazing miracle by our Lord, showing the glory of our Lord, filling the people with a new faith and bringing their Spirit to a new life. I believe that those who were touched and truly transformed spent the rest of their lives glorifying God, spreading his word and doing his work. It is only if we have been re-born in the spirit that we can spend our life doing God's work. Each time we reach out to a widow or orphan in need out of compassion, we visit the sick, we feed the hungry or clothe the naked, may they be amazed at the love that the Lord has for them in providing for their needs and our prayer is that this amazement bring them to a new true faith and a new life in the Spirit.

Luke 8; 49-56 While Jesus was still speaking, someone from the ruler's house came and said, "Your daughter is dead; do not trouble the Teacher anymore." But Jesus on hearing this answered him, "Do not fear; only believe and she will be well." And when he came to the house he allowed no one to enter with him, except Peter and John and James, and the father and mother of the child. And all were weeping and mourning for her, but he said, "Do not weep, for she is not dead but sleeping." And they laughed at him, knowing that she was dead. But taking her by the hand, he called, saying, "Child, arise." And her spirit returned, and she got up at once. And he directed that something should be given her to eat. And her parents were amazed, but he charged them to tell no one what had happened.

In the story of Jairus's daughter, we see how her parents were astounded by her being raised back to life, even today as we speak our Lord restores life in the flesh to many and till today we remain astounded each time an individual is given a new breath of life after we have given them up for dead, our astonishment at the wonders that our Lord continues to perform even till today is only useful to us in as much as it brings us to repentance of sin, a re-birth of the spirit and a new life in Christ.

John 11;3-7, 20-27, 40-44 So the two sisters sent a message to Jesus telling him, "Lord your dear friend is very sick." But when Jesus heard about it he said, "Lazarus's sickness will not end in death.

No, it happened for the glory of God so that the son of God will receive glory from this." So although Jesus loved Martha, Mary and Lazarus, he stayed where he was for the next two days. Finally, he said to his disciples 'Let's go back to Judea. When Martha got word that Jesus was coming she went to meet him. But Mary stayed in the house. Martha said to Jesus,"Lord if only you had been here, my brother would not have died. But even now I know that God will give you whatever you ask. Jesus told her, "Your brother will rise again." 'Yes', Martha said, "He will rise when everybody rises at the last day." Jesus told her, I am the resurrection and the life. Anyone who believes in me will live, even after dying. Everyone who lives in me and believes in me will never ever die. Do you believe this, Martha? "Yes, Lord" she told him. "I have always believed you are the Messiah, the son of God, the one who has come into the world from God. Jesus responded, "Didn't I tell you that you would see God's glory if you believe? So they rolled the stone aside. Then Jesus looked up to heaven and said, "Father, thank you for hearing me. You always hear me, but I said it out for the sake of all these people standing here, so that they will believe you sent me." Then Jesus shouted, "Lazarus, come out!" And the dead man came out, his hands and his feet bound in grave clothes, his face wrapped in a head cloth, Jesus told them, "Unwrap him and let him go."

The story of Lazarus again illustrates our Lord giving life to an individual who had been dead, the resurrection of the dead is a critical doctrine in Christianity, one of the corner stones on which our faith is founded. In fact, if you do not believe in the resurrection of the dead, you cannot be Christian, for if there is no resurrection then our faith has no foundation. The very essence of our faith is that Christ died in reparation of our sins and resurrected in glory to eternal life and if we have this faith we will receive the grace to die to our flesh and rise to a new life in the Spirit so that when our life on earth ends, we do not die. Our hope is that after our resurrection from death and final judgment we return to our heavenly Father's house. If there is no eternal life, then we would have no need to seek eternal life or to be Christian. Martha and Christ enlighten us on the doctrine of the resurrection as Christ refers to himself as the resurrection and the life. We have to live in Christ, giving up our flesh and taking up his Spirit and all this is possible only through the grace that our faith brings us. The raising from the dead of Lazarus is different from the previous illustrations because Lazarus was a personal friend, well known to Christ even before his death. Christ was moved to tears when he felt the pain that his friend Lazarus had suffered before his death, or perhaps he again experienced the pain that his own crucifixion will bring, as in the agony in the garden Christ was moved to tears at the suffering and death of his friend which he only allowed for the greater glory of our Lord, and to win his sheep back into his fold. We must always testify of our healing and opportunity of new life and take the opportunity to share the amazement that wins souls to a new life in Christ. It was definitely out of the compassion in his heart as well as to reveal the glory of God and to give a new life to his followers that Christ gave life to Lazarus. Surely the purpose of God's glory was met as many who had witnessed this miracle of Lazarus's resurrection came to have faith in Christ as the son of God, this faith would bring them the grace that wins us a new life in the Spirit. As Lazarus rose from the dead in flesh the believers were re-born to a new life in Christ.

If the Lord performed these miracles so as to minister to the unbelievers who surrounded him then we must view the resurrection of Christ as the greatest miracle that brings us to

Christ in repentance and wins us a new life in Christ. It is only as we return to the cross in humility and faith that we can be washed clean of our sins and re-born in a new life in the Spirit. Our prayer is that every day we gain true believers that are amazed at the resurrection of Christ and that the faith that this amazement brings leads us all to experience the transformation that is necessary to make us true children of God.

Please join me as I return to the foot of the cross, that we all may be re-born to a new life in Christ Jesus. We must return to Christ repentant and allow ourselves to be washed clean by the waters of baptism. As we receive the grace of the Holy Spirit within our hearts, we must allow him to transform us to children of the Spirit, no longer seeking to indulge our flesh and its needs but rather dying to self and submitting fully to the will of our heavenly father. As children of God we have the power to create new life if we co-operate with our Lord. It is only if we are willing that the creation of each of us as a new being can begin. The freedom is ours to surrender and allow ourselves to be transformed. Unfortunately, we too often allow our desires stand in the way of our salvation. If we are not willing to give up the needs or wants of the flesh that are against our Lord's purpose for creating us, then how can we begin the transformation that makes us children of God. If our faith was even the size of a mustard seed, we would surely give up all of our needs and trade them for eternal life, if that is what it takes. If our faith is real, we would definitely give up all of our earthly possessions to purchase the gift of eternal life, if that is what it takes. There is no doubt that a faith that is real in our one true God is all that is necessary for us to receive the salvation that is ours freely. With a true faith nothing can be allowed to stand in the path of our transformation. If our faith is true then let us all arise, repent and return to our father's house, let us answer the call of salvation as we give up the flesh and its needs. We all are one in the spirit of Christ and the communion of Saints, it is necessary that the love we share causes us to reach out to each other times of need and pray for each other at all times.

Let us pray together:

O Lord our great and compassionate savior, you love us so much you gave up your life for our salvation. Yet we allow our own selfish desires stand in the path of the salvation you earned us. Out of the love you have for us, you have not turned your back on us. You continue to await the return of each of us sinners with open arms, on your cross crucified. All you ask is that we come freely as you speak these words clearly

Let those who hunger, come eat of living bread
Let those who thirst, come drink of living waters
Let those who are in despair, come receive hope
Let those who are depressed, come find joy
Let those who are lost, come be found
Let those who seek, come and find truth
If you feel rejected, come and be accepted
If you've been turned away, come and be welcomed
If you are overburdened come and be lightened of load
If you've been refused come and receive
If you've been abandoned, come and belong
If you are desolate, come be amongst
Those who are confused, come so as to understand
Those who are angry, come so as to be pacified
Those who are weak, come to be strengthened

Those who have been ignored come and be acknowledged
Those who live in sin, come to live in true repentance
Those who continue to seek to fulfill the desires of the flesh, come
to receive the grace of the Holy Spirit
And those who have lost the battle come and win the war
And those who mourn come be comforted
And those who are in pain, come and be consoled
And all the sick, come and be healed
And if everyone has given up on you, come and be lifted up
And those who are hardened of heart come and receive a true love
that heals
Come to me your Lord Jesus Christ as I await you with open arms,
Come as you are, and I will accept you says our Lord and savior
If you ask me, I will forgive you
And if you have faith in me, I will bring you to a new life in the Spirit
that will transform you
Where old things are passed away and my grace is sufficient for
you to win every battle
And you will be my servant and with my Holy Spirit within you,
You will renew the face of the earth with your love
Come and receive freely of the salvation that my death has
earned you
Come and rise to a new life as I empower you with the Spirit that
gives you victory over the flesh.